THE DISSIMULATING HARMONY

THE
DISSIMULATING
HARMONY

The Image of Interpretation in
NIETZSCHE, RILKE, ARTAUD,
and BENJAMIN

CAROL JACOBS

THE JOHNS HOPKINS UNIVERSITY PRESS
Baltimore and London

This book has been brought to publication with the generous
assistance of the Andrew W. Mellon Foundation.

Manufactured in the United States of America

The Johns Hopkins University Press, Baltimore, Maryland 21218
The Johns Hopkins Press, Ltd., London

Library of Congress Catalog Number 77-18392
ISBN 0-8018-2040-5

Library of Congress Cataloging in Publication data
will be found on the last printed page of this book.

CONTENTS

FOREWORD

I well remember that, some ten years ago, I had occasion to recommend to an enlightened and benevolent university press the publication of a dissertation that, in my view, had merits of originality and of critical insight. It dealt with one particular, rather brief work of a very prolific novelist. It was refused for entirely legitimate (though probably misguided) considerations, because the market could not absorb a book-length study of a single work out of a large canon, especially in the case of a novelist. One could justify a book on Flaubert, say, or on Stendhal, but the public would balk at a volume devoted only to *Novembre,* or to *Henry Brulard.* Shortly afterward, Roland Barthes published *S/Z,* which deals, at some length, with a single short story, and his talent and prestige carried the day for a different type and format of critical essay.

Times have changed, and the publication of books like this one bears witness to renewed possibilities of serious and scrupulous work. Consequently, the expectations of the audience likely to read such a book will also have to undergo some modifications. The publisher's attitude in 1967 was symptomatic of what used to be expected from a critical study—and of what will always remain its principal, though perhaps no longer its only, function. On preparing to read a volume that mentions Nietzsche, Rilke, Artaud, and Benjamin on its title page, one expects a contribution to the general understanding of these prominent authors, in the form either of new data about their history or of original, temporarily definitive readings of their main texts, thoughtfully placed within the context of their complete works. One also expects a justification of this particular grouping of writers, a shared theme or motif or predicament that makes their combined study particularly enlightening, or the usual rationale for comparative studies as giving access to a more refined and universal way of writing literary history. One would certainly expect the book to have something to say about the modernity of these authors (since they are all considered to be, in various ways, innovators) or about the nature of their particular alienations and nostalgias, since they were conspicuous outsiders, and some of them were declared insane.

If these broad characterizations may seem to apply less to Rilke than to the others—since he was publicly highly successful and lived what could be considered, from outward appearances, an exemplary and enviably "poetic" life—then one might perhaps speculate how the three others could be played off against Rilke in what would lead to a diagnosis, positive or negative, of the relationships between literature, society, and history.

At the very least, one would expect the essays to reflect, in their style and in their implicit values, the aesthetic pleasure that is bound to be produced by writers of such considerable gifts, all of them remarkable stylists who, by a consensus that no person of taste would wish to question, write very well and attach great importance to formal effects and devices. The readings should respond to the seductiveness of these devices and be, in fact, guided by them. This combination of aesthetic and historical values, despite their apparent independence from each other, grounds in fact the implicit ontology (or metaphysical specificity) of the literary work under which we operate. It determines how we read, how literature is taught in schools and universities, and how the literary commodity is rated in the marketplace. Such a combination of pleasure and worth (history being predestined, by definition, to be hard-working and severe, but responsible) is almost too good to be true and should certainly not be jettisoned lightly.

Coming to *The Dissimulating Harmony* with such expectations one is likely to be disappointed. Historical and psychological considerations are sparse, as are all synthetic judgments about the authors as a group, about each of them individually, and even about the works that Carol Jacobs has selected for analysis. Neither are the essays easy to read or particularly elegant in the conventional sense. They are quite technical and all appear frustratingly inconclusive, leaving us suspended with unresolved difficulties rather than enriched by a new understanding. They are also strikingly self-conscious, more concerned with the predicament of the commentator than with the intrinsic dimensions of the works or the existential pathos of their creation. What then is at stake here? The author's competence is not in question; some historical observations along the way and some paragraphs in which a more subjective voice is heard demonstrate that she could be very successful at a different, more familiar kind of literary criticism. In the name of what considerations does she forgo possibilities of critical discourse that seem easily available to her and to which her subject matter lends itself exceptionally well? One should perhaps not conclude too soon that it is out of perversity or because the contingencies of her literary education deprived her of happier influences.

A speedy way to at least broach what could become a very far-reaching question is to turn to what Jacobs, in her chapter on Rilke, has to say about paraphrase. Paraphrase is, of course, the mainstay of all critical writing. It is generally, though not necessarily, shorter than the text it claims to elucidate, but what is certain is that it can never be exactly the same. It is always a transposition, a translation from "a situation into a *more familiar* situation . . . , something new expressed in the language of something old and familiar." Paraphrase is, therefore, as in the passage from Nietzsche just quoted, a synonym (or a paraphrase) for understanding. It proceeds by a complex and, in the case of a skillful reader, subtle strategy of expansion and elision, the most important being not so much what one develops, makes explicit, and repeats, but what one omits. The principle of omission is usually quite simple: one omits what one does not understand. Since the author has probably done the same thing, concealing and diverting what stands in the way of his own meaning, the complicity between writer, explicator, and reader is particularly effective. In the name of the integrity of the text—a notion to be understood semantically as a potential singularity of meaning, as well as aesthetically and ethically as the coherence and the good faith of the work—whatever stands in the way of this integrity must be erased. The quality of an interpreter is confirmed by his ability to overlook obstacles to understanding. These obstacles are not always the obvious ones; on the contrary, the tactics of paraphrase consist of facing up to apparent difficulties (be they of syntax, of figuration, or of experience) and of coping with them exhaustively and convincingly. Paraphrase is the best way to distract the mind from genuine obstacles and to gain approval, replacing the burden of understanding with the mimicry of its performance. Its purpose is to blur, confound, and hide discontinuities and disruptions in the homogeneity of its own discourse. The precision of what is being said is not taken too seriously. Is it not, after all, the privilege of the arts, as opposed to the sciences, to play freely with truth and falsehood for the sake of graceful effect?

What would happen if, for once, one were to reverse the ethos of explication and try to be really precise, replacing (or at least trying to replace) paraphrase by what one would have to call genuinely analytical reading, just to see what would ensue? Carol Jacobs's work gives a glimpse of some of the consequences. They are quite unsettling, unless of course the reader tries to paraphrase in his turn Carol Jacobs out of the disasters of her own making, explaining her away in ways that are all too easy to imagine. But if one takes her at her word and tries to read her the way she tries to read her texts, surprising things become evident—and not only with reference to these particular texts, though they certainly do not remain untouched. Many assumptions about the still fundamentally dialectical pattern of Nietzsche's thought, about the prophetic authority of Rilke's poetry, about the depth of the nostalgias that allow Benjamin to assert a historical palingenesis beyond the most radical negations, will no longer be so easy to maintain. Readers of Nietzsche, Rilke, Artaud, and Benjamin will have to decide this for themselves by following Jacobs's reading in detail and by testing in very specific ways whether their own assurances and preconceptions are being dislodged by what she brings out. I, for one, admit to having been thus affected and wish to reflect on the general implications of this experience rather than on its consequences for a given author or text, or on the techniques here used to attempt a reading that would no longer blindly submit to the teleology of controlled meaning. All this would have to be the object of a genuine discussion rather than of a brief introduction. But since it is one of Carol Jacobs's virtues to be admirably discreet about the wider implications of her analytical labors, I feel free to state more crudely some of the things that remain delicately implied.

First of all, consider what was referred to as the ethos of this type of discourse. It would be a mistake to assume, because the readings are technical rather than aesthetically pleasing and because they disrupt some of the assertions that have traditionally excited the admiration of many readers, that this critical reader lacks aesthetic sensitivity or ethical concern. She could not begin to write the way she does if she were not keenly responsive to both. The point is rather whether the epistemology of understanding should be predicated by ethical or aesthetic considerations or the other way round. Is the integrity of understanding a function of the integrity of meaning, or should meaning be allowed to disintegrate under the negative impact of elements in a text, however marginal or apparently trivial, that can only be silenced by suppression? Whatever the answer, the conflict is that of one mode of integrity or sensibility with another, and not a priori proof of its absence in the un-doer (nor, for that matter, of its presence in the defender) of the text's stability. Jacobs tries to proceed regardless of the consequences of the understanding she reaches and to be guided first of all by the need for this understanding whatever it may turn out to be—including the hard-earned conviction of its impossibility. In this way, what she wishes is no longer paraphrase but actual reading, productive of its own ethical imperative.

By putting the question thus, it should be clear that there is in fact no real question to be put. For how could a text have its understanding depend on considerations that would not be epistemologically determined? All depends on how one "understands" the relationships between truth and understanding. Understanding is not a version of one single and universal Truth that would exist as an essence, a hypostasis. The truth of a text is a much more empirical and literal event. What makes a reading more or less true is simply the predictability, the necessity of its occurrence, regardless of the reader or of the author's wishes. "Es ereignet sich aber das Wahre" (not *die Wahrheit*) says Hölderlin, which can be freely translated, "What is true is what is bound to take place." And, in the case of the reading of a text, what takes place is a necessary understanding. What marks the truth of such an understanding is not some abstract universal but the fact that it has to occur regardless of other considerations. It depends, in other words, on the rigor of the reading as argument. Reading is an argument (which is not necessarily the same as a polemic) because it has to go against the grain of what one would want to happen in the name of what has to happen; this is the same as saying that understanding is an epistemological event prior to being an ethical or aesthetic value. This does not mean that there can be a true reading, but that no reading is conceivable in which the question of its truth or falsehood is not primarily involved.

It would therefore be naive to make a reading depend on considerations, ethical or aesthetic, that are in fact correlatives of the understanding the reading is able to achieve. Naive, because it is not a matter of choice to omit or to accentuate by paraphrase certain elements in a text at the expense of others. We don't have this choice, since the text imposes its own understanding and shapes the reader's evasions. The more one censors, the more one reveals what is being effaced. A paraphrase is always what we called an analytical reading, that is, it is always susceptible of being made to point out consistently what it was trying to conceal. Knowing this, the difference between Carol Jacobs and other critics (who presumably write paraphrases without worrying about it) is not so great after all, since all of us are always doing what she is doing, whether we know it or not. But once we know it, we cannot go back to our original innocence, for one has to be quite smart in order to pretend convincingly to be dumb.

So, in one respect, the interest of Jacobs's way of reading is that she does openly what we have no choice but to do anyway, when our most cherished certainties about Nietzsche, say, or about Rilke or about ourselves are being dissolved by understanding. But this is only one perspective upon a tale that does not stop there. This argument has driven us into a corner, a bind that has to do, as it happens, with the nature of arguments. True reading, as opposed to paraphrase, is an argument, that is, it has the sequential coherence we associate with a demonstration or with a particularly compelling narrative. But what is here being argued (or compellingly told) is precisely the loss of an illusory coherence: the historical consistency of Nietzsche's theory of tragedy or the existential necessity of Rilke's fulfillment by renunciation or Artaud's fulfillment by cruelty, etc.

The argument, assuming it resists attempts to find fault with the details of its articulation, demonstrates the necessary occurrence of this disruption and, what is more, designates it by a variety of specific names: *stammering, beheading,* and finally, the *image.* These names are not arbitrary but are literally present in the texts, though muted or disguised: the word *stammer* occurs in Nietzsche in places now shown to be crucial; beheading and castration are explicit in Rilke, albeit disguised at times by various plays of the signifier; *image (Bild)* is, like the purloined letter, so literally inscribed in Benjamin's diction (and even in one of his titles) that no one seems to have noticed it until Jacobs came along. This sequence of terms clinches, as the saying goes, the argument, in a well-modulated progression that leads ir-resistibly to the key term, *image. Image* is now shown to be the term that subsumes the others, and *stammering, beheading,* etc., proven to be mere images for *image.* By the same token, the demonstration of this necessary incoherence becomes a remarkably sound narrative, and the entire book can be summarized in the single parable of the last chapter: not just the tale of Rastelli the juggler as told by Benjamin's fictional narrator, but this tale plus the added turn that Carol Jacobs's commentary gives to it. Reading becomes a parable *(Gleichnis)*, an allegory of reading as the literal designation of its undoing.

But how is it possible for a literal designation to be an image, that which is never literal? What these essays convincingly demonstrate is that the disruption of meaning occurs when the literal or figural status of the text's central event (its understanding) has to be, and cannot be, decided. What is here astutely called *image* is the necessity for any literal, and therefore comprehensible, meaning to be disguised in a representation that can be called a history, a narrative, an argument, a parable, or an allegory, but that errs to the exact extent that it represents. One will have recognized the not-so-secret theme of Nietzsche's *The Birth of Tragedy*. But whereas the apparent fluidity of Nietzsche's text turns out to be a stammer, the high quality of Carol Jacobs's readings threaten her with a worse danger. She cannot prevent her stammering text from being impeccably fluid. Parable turns into paraphrase after all, even and especially when one is as fully aware as she is of this inconsistency. The result is no longer the birth of something purely tragic, though it is certainly not benign. It may well be the birth of criticism as truly critical reading, a birth that is forever aborted and forever repeated but that, in the meantime, makes for indispensable reading.

PAUL DE MAN

PREFACE

The Task of the Interpreter

The essays that follow could well be interpreted as placing the identical question. But they will no less place the identical in question and therefore, of necessity, place in question the truth-value of the preface that attempts to create the fictional basis for their common origin. That identical question, which indeed presupposes the possibility of a certain identity: "What is the Image?"

What is the image in the fragments of the studies preliminary to *The Birth of Tragedy*, in *The Theater and Its Double* and *Héliogabale*, in Rilke's tenth *Duino Elegy*, and in Benjamin's essay on Proust?

In the case of Nietzsche, any definition of the image or symbol turns on the possibility of reifying the distinction between the Apollonian and the Dionysian. And yet the Apollonian—the plastic representational image, that which gives measure and the knowledge of clear boundaries and which, in its Socratic intensification, becomes conceptual and theoretical language—cannot, in the final analysis, be distinguished from the oblivion and original contradiction of the Dionysian. As Nietzsche elaborates the long history determined by the interrelationship between these two aesthetic drives, they turn about one another in an eternal reversal that perpetually undermines the ground for a definitive differentiation.

In the tenth *Duino Elegy*, Rilke dissimulates the nature of the image. The poem is organized to suggest an apotheosis of that language which sacrifices immediate presence for higher meaning. But the last eight lines of the elegy upset the possibility of this simple coincidence of language and meaning by introducing the startling notion of the *Gleichnis* (image, simile, comparison, parable).

Initiation into the image of *Héliogabale* takes place by way of the "hieroglyph" (*The Theater and Its Double*): for the hieroglyph, as an endless series of violent displacements from the origin it pretends to name, demystifies Artaud's pretence of a return to concrete reality through language. It is this figure that can be seen to govern the entire textuality of *Héliogabale,* a text comprised of 'themes' analogous to that of the hieroglyph—the question of the obliterated origin of Héliogabale (and implicitly *Héliogabale*), the historical framework as a *démarquage* that perpetually obscures the mark of that which it copies, the temple structures as endless spirals of similar but mutually canceling layers, the dislocation of the voice of Logos in the tale of Palamedes, and the repeated menace of the apocalypse of the sign.

And what of Benjamin? It is his text that speaks most directly to the problematic, for its title, "Towards the Image of Proust," openly proclaims its concern with metaphor, and a definition of the image, however opaque and enigmatic, is registered in the opening paragraph. Yet this definition, which describes the image as marking a discrepancy between language and life, not only denies the recuperation promised by Proust's *mémoire involontaire,* but undermines the biographical and referential rhetoric of Benjamin's own text.

The chain of deconstructions cannot, of course, be contained here: for if the image functions as a violent displacement from the origin, life, or meaning to which it apparently refers, there is a second fundamental question raised more or less explicitly in each of these essays. What about my text as the image of the image: what about the possibility of reading or interpretation? At this juncture, according to Nietzsche, I can only stammer in a language which, while repeating its textual object, renders it incomprehensible. According to Rilke, the reader is hurled from the transcendent heights of apparent understanding. According to Artaud, this question is answered by the anarchical laughter of the literary text as it imposes its deceptions on the interpreter. I elaborate on this predicament at the end of my essay on Benjamin: it is repeated once again in the Afterword—"I, the Juggler"—which is, perhaps, Benjamin's essay on me.

* * *

Benjamin's essay, "The Task of the Translator," is a translation of the notion of translation. Here translation may appear to mean 'translation,' but it is in the nature of translation to presuppose other, foreign, meanings. Thus translation functions as a metaphor both for the potential text-ness of a text and also as a metaphor for that which

Benjamin calls "criticism." It is this kind of criticism, in which the text-ness of the text is given full play, that I hope to have written. To be sure, a certain monstrousness may be sensed in this type of interpretation. Benjamin, who repeatedly speaks of Hölderlin's translations as the most perfect of their kind, also calls them monstrous examples of literalness.

> Literality thoroughly overthrows all reproduction of meaning with regard to the syntax and threatens directly to lead to incomprehensibility. In the eyes of the nineteenth century, Hölderlin's translations of Sophocles were monstrous examples of such literality.... [T]he demand for literality is no offspring of an interest in maintaining meaning. [*Gesammelte Schriften* (Frankfurt: Suhrkamp, 1972), IV:1, pp. 17–18.]

This monstrousness of literal (in Benjamin's sense of the word) reading is admittedly at play in the pages that follow.

I am grateful to those who so generously and perceptively performed the task of commentary: Paul de Man, Richard Macksey, J. Hillis Miller.

NOTE: Translations appear at the foot of pertinent text pages as unnumbered footnotes.

NIETZSCHE

The Stammering Text: The Fragmentary Studies
Preliminary to *The Birth of Tragedy*

CHAPTER ONE

The time is out of joint.—Hamlet, *I,v.*

Dionysus speaks the language of Apollo, but Apollo finally [speaks] the language of Dionysus.—The Birth of Tragedy *I: 120.*

... almost undecided as to whether it will communicate or conceal, as if stammering in a foreign tongue.—The Birth of Tragedy *I: 12.*

[C]onsequently the reassuring dichotomy between the metaphorical and the proper is exploded, that dichotomy in which each member of the pair never did more than reflect the other and direct back its radiance.—Jacques Derrida, "White Mythology," New Literary History *(1974), VI: 74.*

Since a fragmentary text[1] offers innumerable points of departure, it is perhaps most expedient to tell a story. In this way, we at least create for ourselves the illusion that a beginning and an end are to be found. It will be a historical story, one that we read many times in Nietzsche, although it may later show itself to be a mythical story: "the historical facts are dissolved into free myth-substances"[2] (9[58]).[3] A history therefore, a chain of events, but as a totality this history serves as an interpretation of the ninth notebook of the studies preliminary to *The Birth of Tragedy*, at least *one* possible interpretation. Nietzsche wrote this chronicle repeatedly: we will do so once again by seeking out and piecing together the different periods as they appear in the fragments: Music / Tragedy / Socrates / Wagner—"a succession of images" (9[125]), that will allow us to deal with a far more complex web of images—birth, history/story, image, imitation, model, morality, metaphor, character, convulsion, stammering.

The clearest scheme outlined by the notebook is that tragedy is born out of music, that Socratic thought then marks the death of tragedy, and that Wagner in turn overcomes the Socratic opera, bringing about a rebirth of music.

The birth of tragedy out of music. 9[2]
The dissolution of music into myth is the tragic. 9[125]

Socratism conquers the myth. 9[58]
Death of tragedy, together with a continued life as mystery.
The genius of science kills it [tragedy].
But even Socrates is in doubt.[4] 9[38]

Wagner has brought the original tendency of the opera to its consequences. . . . Wagner tries simply to cast down the Atlas of modern cul-
ture: his music imitates the original music. 9[149]

This historical chain seems smooth enough: yet our concern will be
to designate the constellation of images that articulate the links, an
articulation which proves to be rather problematical. To read the text
in such a manner, we are forced to jump continually about—a bit
convulsively—from a particular fragment to one similar to it, the second almost repeating the first, but also interpreting it. We can only
hope that this frenetic reading will not entirely displace the meaning
of the text.

The model for the articulation between two historical periods is, of
course, the birth of tragedy out of music. We will read at first simply
in order to fix "the nomenclature of the events"(9[42]).

The Dionysian as mother . . . of tragedy. 9[61]

The ancient myth is usually born from music. A succession of images.
These are the *tragic* myths. 9[125]

Out of the Dionysian world the image comes to light. Metamorphosis
into the *Myth*.
The *tragic* tendency as a result of the spirit of music. 9[31]
The *ancient tragedy*: the chorus which dreamed an Apollonian dream.
9[90]

From the *Dionysian*, from the spirit of *music*, from the chorus on the
one hand, *tragedy*, the *image*, the *myth*, the *Apollonian* dream are produced. Now we, along with Nietzsche, must place the fundamental
question: "What is the relationship of the two aesthetic drives
[*Kunsttriebe*] to one another?" (9[36]) (the relationship between the
Dionysian, music and the chorus on the one hand and the Apollonian,
the image and the myth on the other), for, "This explains the birth of
tragedy" (9[36]).

This movement from the one to the other, from the Dionysian
chorus to tragedy, can be traced through three passages.

The scene and its action can be explained only from the standpoint of the *chorus*. It is only in so far as the chorus is only the representation of the reveling Dionysian masses, only in so far as every spectator identifies himself with the chorus, that there is a spectator-world in the Greek theater. Schlegel's phrase about the "ideal spectator" must open for us here a much deeper meaning. The chorus is the idealized spectator [*Zuschauer*], in so far as he is the only beholder [*Schauer* which also means shudder, spasm], the beholder of the visionary world of the scene. He is the actual *engenderer* of that world: nothing is more erroneous than to attribute our standard of the aestheticizing critical audience to the Greek theater. The Dionysian masses as the eternal natal womb of the Dionysian manifestation [*Erscheinung*]—and here the eternally unfruitful— that is the contradiction. 9[9]

The chorus as a representation of the Dionysian masses engenders the visionary world of the scene: it is the only *Schauer* (beholder/ spasm) in the double sense of the word—both the convulsion of the body that serves as the birth spasm of tragedy, therefore the origin of the vision—as well as the beholder of a vision that has always been located outside of him. The Dionysian masses are characterized by a contradiction: they are not only "the eternal natal womb of the Dionysian manifestation"—thus, apparently, eternally fruitful—but also "the eternally unfruitful." They are the eternally fruitful womb of the Dionysian manifestation, since music continually suffers fruitful birth pangs—the eternally unfruitful, since this "Dionysian manifestation" is never presented as *Dionysian,* but rather as Apollonian. "Music incites to the *symbolical* [*gleichnisartigen*] *contemplation* of the Dionysian universality. Music, then, lets the symbolical [Apollonian][5] image . . . arise" (*The Birth of Tragedy*, I: 92). The attempt to produce an exact Dionysian copy of the Dionysian engenderer always runs up against a certain impediment.

Two other passages repeat the same patterns by which the Apollonian is generated.

Two different points of departure of the Greek *tragedy*: the chorus which sees a vision and the enchanted Dionysian improvisor. The chorus explains only the *living image*: the improvisor explains the *drama*.

The *melting together of the vision with the enchanted improvisation*—origin of the drama. 9[104]

This improvisation entails the "projection of images" (8[7])[6] which the chorus brings about (cf. 9[9]), and we see it described elsewhere (in

9[105]) as the production of character (the other point of departure of tragedy).

> What kind of capability is it to *improvise from the standpoint of an unknown character?* It is certainly not a question of imitation, for it is not reflection that is the origin of such improvisations. Really the thing to ask is—how is it possible to *enter into an unknown personality?* 9[105]

The improvisation from the standpoint of an unknown character cannot be called imitation, for the gesture that produces improvisation comes from the rending of music within itself and not from its mimesis by means of an image brought from the outside.

> This is first of all a liberation from one's own personality, that is, a sinking of oneself into a representation. Here we see how the representation is capable of differentiating the expressions of the will, how all character is an internal representation. This internal representation is obviously not identical with our conscious thinking about ourselves.
>
> Now this entering into an unknown personality is also an *aesthetic pleasure:* that is, the expressions of the will, through a *continually deepening* representation, finally become different, that is, differentiated, and are finally made silent.
>
> The *disguise [Verstellung]* in the service of egoism also shows the power of representation to differentiate the expressions of the will. 9[105]

The engendering of character takes place in a schismatic description—in the cleft between a terminology of interiority (sinking oneself, internal, entering into, deepening) and of exteriority (liberation, representation, differentiating, expressions). Entering into an unknown character takes place by sinking oneself into an internal representation. We should not let the apparent simplicity of this description deceive us, for here a violent rending of the will takes place. The expressions of the will, of the Dionysian life of impulse, are differentiated, so very differentiated in their projection that these expressions become disguised, that is, they are "finally different," "finally made silent."

The Dionysian is silenced, for no sooner has the violent self-rending of the Dionysian spirit of music engendered the character, than this character takes on the appearance of something entirely exterior, something coming from the outside, something which has been "poured out over our life of impulse."

> Character seems therefore to be a representation that has been poured out over our life of impulse, a representation in which all expressions of

that life come to light. This representation is appearance and that life of impulse is the truth, the eternal—whereas the appearance is the transient. The will [is] the general, the representation that which differentiates. 9[105]

But perhaps we have committed the error of pushing things too far, since we find ourselves already at the limits of tragedy. We wanted to follow the birth of tragedy out of music—from the chorus that sees a vision, from the will or life of impulse to the improvisation, in order to bring forth the Apollonian character, which, thus fused together with the Dionysian, was supposed to constitute tragedy. Yet we have already overstepped the threshold of synthesis to emerge on the side of the purely Apollonian: "*Character* is a typical representation of the originary unity, a representation which, however, we come to know only as a multiplicity of expressions."

Two things must be kept in mind. First, that this Apollonian representation can be known only as "expressions"—therefore as images or words. Second, that this representation is a presentation of the will—but a false presentation. Thus Nietzsche calls it a "disguise," for it presents the will as an originary unity, the very will that we have seen to be already in the process of differentiating itself.

The disguised representation mentioned in fragment 105 (the tragic myth, the series of images that are born out of music), Nietzsche calls elsewhere "interpretation of music" (9[125]). This interpretation plays its role as a remedy against the originary pain.

Image and thought are here even more: they break the totally consuming influence of music, they moderate it.—Originary pain. To that extent word and image are a remedy against music: at first word and image bring us closer to music, then they protect us against it.[7] 9[135]

The image moderates the consuming influence of music; it masks the originary pain which we have seen as the differentiation of the expressions of the will and represents this originary pain rather as an originary unity. The image is interpretation of music, but it disguises at the same time that which it presents.

We should not forget, however, although we will inevitably forget it again, that this 'false' representation of music, this interpreting reversal or turning about of music into its apparent opposite,[8] which seems to take place after a fixed musical era, has always been inscribed in the originary contradiction of music itself, and that it is music itself that engenders its own 'false' interpretation. Music's expression of a self-portrait which differentiates itself from itself is yet another expression of the originary contradiction.

At the end of fragment 105, an even greater separation from music as original contradiction takes place.

> Now, that original representation which constitutes character is also the mother of all *moral* phenomena. And that temporary raising up of character (in the aesthetic pleasure, in improvisation) is a transformation of moral character. It is that world of the *best,* which is linked to representation and *appearance* out of which moral phenomena arise. The illusory world of representation, aims at the redemption of the world and its perfection. This perfecting of the world would lie in the destruction of the originary pain and originary contradiction, that is, in the destruction of the essence of things and in appearance alone—therefore in nonbeing.
>
> Everything *good* comes out of the temporary *submersion in representation,* that is out of becoming one with appearance. 9[105]

The same movement that produces the tragic image engenders at the same time the possibility of the death of tragedy, for this representation is also "mother of all moral phenomena," the moral that lies clearly on the side of Socratic thought, of the "death of tragedy" (9[38])—the optimistic Socratic thought which *The Birth of Tragedy* calls correction of the world[9] or its perfection. The temporary establishment of character enables the repression of the painful gesture of differentiation. Character is produced by means of a "temporary submersion" in or "becoming one with appearance," a "destruction of the originary pain and the originary contradiction." We will return to this question later—that of morality and the becoming one with appearance, when we establish morality's relationship to the image, to musical beat and to history.

Our point of departure was the trajectory between the will (chorus or music) and the improvisation of character, that is, a description of the birth of tragedy. But since all limitations on this convulsive chain of birth prove impossible, tragedy has, in turn, engendered Socratic thought. We have unintentionally been cast into the epoch of the Socratic opera, and since we have already discovered its place of birth—namely, in tragedy—we can interpret its development from an internal vantage point.

Improvisation, we have read, is anything but an imitation—rather a convulsive differentiation of the will in bringing forth a representation. However Nietzsche may insist on the fact that this representation is *internal,* it appears, nevertheless, as that which comes from the outside, as image, or imitation—and that which this representation imitates and interprets seems not at all to be the essence of the will as original contradiction. Right there we have the entire story of Socratism—but not Socratism as a historical era, not as the death of tragedy that appears temporally after tragedy from somewhere outside of it, but rather as a potential of tragedy which has always been in the process of differentiating itself: and tragedy, in turn, stood in the same relationship to the will. Indeed, Socratism presents a repetition of tragedy (of certain aspects of its Apollonian manifestation), but it is a repetition which at the same time renders that which is repeated incomprehensible, that reverses everything—thus a convulsive repetition that at the same time appears as contradiction.

If we summarize how Socratism, and in particular the Socratic opera, plays its role, we will understand the era that follows, that of Wagner, all the better. Just as the image, the tragic myth, arose to offer a remedy against the originary contradiction of the Dionysian will, now thought and the word protect against the myth—for in the tragic myth that originary pain was still alive.

> Socratism conquers the myth. . . . The graphic arts perish because of thought. 9[58]
>
> . . . tragedy perished only because of an excessive preference for the Apollonian. 9[10]
>
> The image saves from being entangled in orgiastic moods. . . . *Thought (and the word)* as remedy against the myth. 9[12]

This protection against the myth by means of the word indicates a flight from incomprehensibility, for the goal of the movement out of which opera arose was *"to understand the word"* and "the first consequence of that demand that one understand the singer" was *"that speech be imitated by the song"* (9[5]). The word takes its justified role as master and the song (the music) takes on the role of servant: music is now mere imitation of speech.

The relationship seems clear up to this point. But if we read the tenth fragment, this reversal of the former relationship between the Apollonian and Dionysian no longer appears so simple.

> Complete *reversal* of the relationship between the Dionysian and Apollonian. The Apollonian is *for us that which is understood with difficulty.* We have to interpret the *image* in order to get to the myth. . . . The German talent, which first came to light in Luther, then again in German music

has made us familiar with the Dionysian once again: it is by far the more powerful. In addition, the wisdom of the Dionysian is for us the more familiar form. We are totally incapable of arriving at the naive—with the help of the Apollonian. We can, however, interpret the world purely Dionysically and can explain the world of appearance to ourselves through music. In this way, we at least achieve the aesthetic contemplation of the world, the myth.[10] 9[10]

In the Socratic opera, the word denies that total comprehensibility which was promised. The description of the beginnings of the opera (9[5]) relates how the subservient music imitated the word. Precisely this imitation now seems to be indispensable, for, in contrast to the Greeks, for whom the interpretation of music required the image, for us, the Apollonian is now the incomprehensible, and the interpreting music the indispensable. We interpret the world of appearance of the word or image through music.[11]

Nietzsche traces this inversion of the relationship between music and word still further. The new fragment seems to be a repetition of that which we have just read in the tenth fragment, except that it introduces the new, not insignificant, term "symbol."

> The symbol—in the original period as *language [Sprache]* for the *general*,
> in the later period as a means of remembering the *concept*.
> Music—actually language of the general. In the opera it became used as symbol of the concept. 9[88]

Nietzsche inscribes the symbol doubly into his text, once as the music of the original period, as language of the general, and once again as a degraded means of remembering the concept.

In fragment (9[92]), it is the same story, but told rather confusingly. We find here a convulsive stuttering of the word "symbol," for it, or one of its variations, appears no less than eleven times within nine sentences. Precisely this spasmodic repetition of the term makes the passage unreadable, since this signifier indicates (at least) two contradictory meanings, meanings that we can grasp conceptually thanks to the fragment just read (9[88]): (1) symbol as language of the general and (2) symbol as means of remembering the concept.[12]

> The deficiency of the *symbol* (1 or 2) in our modern world. Understanding the world in *"symbols"* (1) is the precondition of a great art. For us music has become myth, that is, a world of *symbols* (2): we relate to music as the Greek did to his *symbolic* (2) myths.

> A human race which sees the world only abstractly and not in *symbols* (1) is incapable of art. We have the idea in place of the *symbol* (1)—therefore tendentiousness as the aesthetic guiding star.

Now there are men who understand the world as music—that is, symbolically (1). Regarding things musically is a new artistic possibility.

Therefore—to look upon an event—not with respect to the idea that lies within it but with respect to its musical *symbolism* (1): that is the Dionysian *symbolism* (1) will be continually felt in everything. (My italics and, of course, numerals—9[92].)

Indeed, this babble doesn't seem to want to communicate anything beyond that which we already read in fragment (9[10]): in the case of the Greeks, music was explained through the image, now the image is explained through music.

The ancient fable symbolized the Dionysian (in images). Now the Dionysian symbolizes the image. The Dionysian was explained through the image. Now the image is explained through the Dionysian. Therefore completely reversed relationship. How is that possible?—If the image can indeed be a simile of the Dionysian?—The ancients sought to grasp the Dionysian through the simile of the image. We presuppose the Dionysian understanding and seek to grasp the imagistic-simile [*Bildgleichnis*]. We and they compare. They were interested in the simile-quality of the image: we are interested in the general Dionysian.

For them the world of images was the clear world: for us it is the Dionysian. 9[92]

But how is this unthinkable relationship possible?—a relationship in which the image is a simile of the Dionysian and, on the other hand, the Dionysian is a simile for the image. If this were the case, there could be no firm basis for comparison, but rather an eternal reversal in which certain polarizations would indeed take place, but in which the poles are not only opposite one another but also identical. "We and they compare. They were interested in the simile [that is, Apollonian] quality of the image: we are interested in the general Dionysian" quality. For us, the Apollonian image plays the same role as the Dionysian did for the Greeks and the boundless reversibility of roles prevents us from determining where the original Dionysian and Apollonian poles lie.[13]

The game Nietzsche plays with the term "symbol" might have made us suspect that, for the instructive moral of that story related in fragment 92 could be read as follows: *The Symbol Symbolizes the Symbol.* That indicates first of all that the one meaning determines the other meaning: only in so far as a conceptual symbol is thinkable, is its opposite, symbol as language of the general—as the unmediated—definable.

Thus far we have indicated only two opposing meanings of the word "symbol"; yet a third also comes into play—specifically in those sentences which gave us the model for our moral (*The Symbol Symbolizes the Symbol*).

> The ancient fable symbolized the Dionysian (in images). Now the Dionysian symbolizes the image. 9[92]

The *verb*—symbolize—precisely that which designates the trajectory of differentiation of the one symbol from and through the other, cannot be grasped either as a language of pure immediacy or as imitation, although it makes both possible.

Symbolizing—this unceasing movement of eternal reversal[14]—could also be termed "myth." As we traced the trajectory of the birth of tragedy out of music, we often simply identified the term "myth" with the metaphorical. It is not such a simple matter. For in the tenth fragment we found that the reversed trajectory, the trajectory of interpreting the image through music, also brings us to the myth. One arrives at the myth whether starting at one point of departure or the other, and in the myth the unending reversal of both orientations takes place. It makes possible the rupturing differentiation of the simile and obliterates the traces, usually by presenting itself simply as the plastic image.[15]

We turn now to the next historical epoch, that of Wagner, of the death of the Socratic opera. It becomes more and more difficult to continue this historical game, but in order to continue speaking we must not let the mask fall. The opera, as the age of the understandable word, lowered music to the means of representation (9[5]) and through this change, the word became that which was incomprehensible and assumed the former role of music. Now, "Even Socrates is in doubt" (9[38]), for the heroic opera is already a transition into the (Wagnerian) tragedy (9[41]). This confusing reversal of directions that already takes place in the era of the opera explains why Nietzsche over and over emphasizes Wagner's role as perfector of the opera.

> The perfecting of the *idyllic opera tendency* through Wagner. 9[90]

> There was a *German music* in his mind that is liberated from the romantic yoke: this as well as the related German art he finds at first only as a *radical creator of idylls,* as perfector of the romanic thought. 9[135]

For according to Nietzsche's history, Wagner's arrival signifies not simply the return to power of music, which was earlier made to serve the word, but rather the complete reversibility of music and image that we saw to be the final consequences of the opera. This complete reversibility could be called music in a much wider sense. Therefore, Nietzsche can describe the relationship between music (in the limited sense) and image in Wagner in opposite ways. On the one hand, the image as means of representation of a comprehensible story protects against the "consuming influence of music" (9[135]). But precisely because of the fact that language seems to assume the main role, music appears merely as the means to represent the word, and the word thus takes on the character of music.

> The *poetical action* in Wagner—very great. The word doesn't work through prolixity, but through *intensity*. Language is *thought into an origi-nal state*, through music. Therefore the brevity and constriction of ex-pression. 9[72]

The word works as music—rather than as language—through its rhythmical intensity.[16]

Nietzsche describes this phenomenon of reversibility as: "The pro-gress to the symphony in Wagner. A juxtaposition of both worlds without prejudice" (9[90]). This unbiased juxtaposition of the Apol-lonian and Dionysian seems to be anything but that relatively clear succession that our historical scheme presented until now.

> Richard Wagner—the idyll of the present.... We still reach only the idyll. Wagner has pushed the original trend of the opera, the *idyllic* trend, to its consequences: music as idyllic (with a shattering of the forms).... He creates his lyrical roles merely out of his musical moods, therefore they coincide with [*sich decken*—which also means to conceal] one another as a *totality*.... Wagner *chooses* from the music that lives inside him: the characterization is taken from keen observation of the executing singers and musicians. Here lies all the imitation: the designa-tion of tempo "presto" is not absolute but only for the executing musi-cians. The orchestra is thought correspondingly "mimetically": *in the music, conceived as executed, the analogon is sought to the mimicry of the dramatic singers.* Above all, the declamation belongs to this mimicry, to which now a corresponding mimicry of the orchestra corresponds. Thus the or-chestra is merely a strengthening of the mimetic pathos. 9[149]

If the characterization imitates the music of the performing singers, the opposite is no less true. And thus it goes on: music, characteriza-tion, performing singers and musicians, the orchestra, the declamation—each imitates the next and as a totality they all corre-spond to one another. The German verb here is *sich decken* which means not only mutual correspondence but also reciprocal conceal-ment. Wagner's work functions as an endless mimetic echoing of elements, in which no single element can be fixed as the definitive origin of the other, therefore radically threatening the comprehensibility of the whole.

Now we can begin to read the figure of Wagner as something other than a historical phenomenon. In fragment 36, Nietzsche writes:

> For me the phenomenon of Wagner considered corporeally is at first to be negatively interpreted,—namely that up until now we have not understood the Greek world, and, inversely, we find there the only analogies to our phenomenon of Wagner. 9[36]

That could simply mean, although the explanation is not sufficient, that that late phenomenon, Wagner, has not yet pushed things as far as his predecessors, the Greeks. Or, based on our newly acquired knowledge about the nature of the image, we might add that Wagner, as an *analogy* of the Greeks, renders incomprehensible that which he imitates. The word "inversely" makes a third meaning of the sentence almost unreadable. We find an analogy to Wagner in the Greeks precisely *because* both practice the incomprehensible.

And perhaps it has always been this way. This multiple interpretation of fragment 36 is not dissimilar to our experience with history. As we repeated Nietzsche's history of tragedy, we followed it through a linear progression—its birth out of music, its death in the Socratic opera, its rebirth in Wagner. But with the arrival of a new era, we always ran into a particular impediment, and at each point of articulation between two epochs, which always appeared in the form of mimesis, we established an unthinkable juxtaposition of events:

—the new epoch imitates the previous one, as though it were an image coming from the outside.
—the new epoch, precisely by portraying the last epoch, at the same time reverses it and renders it incomprehensible.
—this reversing repetition always has already taken place in the previous epoch itself.

The mimetic echoing of corresponding elements of the Wagnerian opera presented an image of this, a juxtaposition of what was previously described as a temporal succession: there the clear distinction of the two aesthetic drives—the Apollonian and the Dionysian—was no longer possible.

We can now return to Nietzsche's "fundamental question" of passage 36, to a question that will now certainly appear either very naive or very ironical. "Fundamental question: What is the relationship of the two aesthetic drives to one another? This explains the birth of tragedy." (9[36]). We can finally give Nietzsche's direct answer to this question:

> The Greeks help us more than our own aestheticians with their basic distinction between Dionysian and Apollonian. The relationship of the two aesthetic principles is totally without aesthetic principles. This lack of knowledge makes the discussion of Wagner now so difficult. 9[34]

The relationship of the two aesthetic principles on which we based our historical development is totally without principles, totally lacking that which can be set down as a predetermined conceptual law. For it was precisely this historical exposition that brought us to those mimetic reverberations, to the lack of any such Socratic science, to that which Nietzsche calls—lack of knowledge. Therefore, Nietzsche finds it so difficult to speak of Wagner. He can do so only by presenting Wagner as a model (among other models—the Greeks, Shakespeare, etc.), as an instructive historical example, from which one can learn the meaninglessness of the instructive and the historical.[17]

> . . . we are learned artists. Groping for models. There is no more instructive moment than the appearance of Wagner.
>
> In our era, aesthetic phenomena are completely disguised and recognized in an erudite manner. For me the value of Wagner. . . .
>
> The relationship of the two aesthetic principles is totally without aesthetic principles. This lack of knowledge makes the discussion of Wagner now so difficult: to which must be added that the entire liberal world defends itself against the spirit of music and its philosophical interpretation. Music annihilates civilization just as sunlight does lamplight. 9[34]

We can confirm this assertion of the annihilation of civilization, of history, once again in fragment 42. Certainly, we won't *learn* anything from it, but we can at least expand the web of images.

The text offers itself as a historical lesson in aesthetics, but this same gesture reveals the deficiency of knowledge in such a lesson.

> For he, into whose flesh and blood the aesthetic lesson already expounded in this treatise has entered—which implies that the lesson's basis, the facts of the Dionysian and Apollonian, were already present in him in the form of unconscious observations—he who, with us, has been taught and convinced instinctively by the wisest teacher, Nature, about the eternal validity of those two aesthetic drives and their necessary relationships, he may now, with an unobstructed view place himself op-

> posite the analogous phenomena of the present, as a contemplator who
> wants nothing for himself but who seeks the truth for the entire world.
> 9[42]

Nietzsche's text was incapable of teaching us anything that wasn't
already in us. It speaks, to be sure, about the "necessary relationships"
of the two aesthetic drives: we know, however, that any knowledge of
these is out of the question—from the very beginning. And this passage has no other intention than to once again communicate this lack
of knowledge. Nietzsche assumes the mask of objectivity, and we, the
reader, must also play the role of the philosopher.[18]

> For he, into whose flesh and blood the aesthetic lesson already ex-
> pounded in this treatise has entered.... he may now, with an un-
> obstructed view place himself opposite the analogous phenomena of the
> present, as a contemplator who wants nothing for himself but who seeks
> the truth for the entire world. He has already tested and strengthened
> his glance on a series of historical pasts and must now demand to also get
> a word in with respect to reality. 9[42]

This phrase, "to get a word in," must be taken quite literally. For in
contemplating reality, as with history, one finds nothing other than
words: here there is nothing other than the example and exemplify-
ing, in short, a mimetic repetition with contradiction and never a
scientific knowledge of the matter.

> History, of course, never teaches directly, it only demonstrates with
> examples. And even the reality present around us cannot help us attain
> any deeper knowledge, but rather simply confirms and exemplifies that
> knowledge. I would like to call out precisely to our era with its "objec-
> tive," indeed absolute conduct of historical writing, that this "objectivity"
> is merely dreamed up, and that it is rather the case that even those
> historical writings—in so far as they are not dry collections of
> documents—signifiy nothing other than a collection of examples for
> general philosophical propositions. . . .
>
> It is only for the disinterested eyes of the philosopher that history re-
> flects eternal laws, while [and here Nietzsche describes his own text] the
> man who stands in the midst of the flow of the egotistical will, when he
> has reasons to take up the mask of objectivity, must resign himself to
> gnaw with offensive thoroughness on the nomenclature of the events
> and, as it were, the outermost rind—whereas, on the other hand, with
> every expanded judgment that he makes, he exposes his philosophically
> crude understanding of the world which is inaccessible to any deeper
> contemplation of self and therefore indifferent. 9[42]

Nietzsche, therefore, assumes the mask of objectivity, the nomenclature of historical events, so that each judgment may show how incapable it is to bring us to true knowledge.

> Totally disregarding this historical "method" and its advocates, let us place ourselves with our aesthetic knowledge in the midst of the aesthetic present in order to explain it with that knowledge—to which end it is immediately necessary to lay stress on several manifestations of this present and to prove them worthy of explanation. 9[42]

As though wishing once again to exemplify this donning of the mask of objectivity, Nietzsche suggests that we explain our aesthetic present with our aesthetic knowledge—as though he had already forgotten that "the reality present around us cannot help us attain any deeper knowledge, but rather simply confirms and exemplifies" history. That which we may expect from these manifestations of the present, therefore, is nothing other than exemplification and illustration, or images of images.

> Let us think of the fate of the best known Shakesperian drama in our theaters. I have always noted among the better educated spectators a unique perplexity with respect to this drama. All of these were conscious of having gained for themselves, from their intimate, deep acquaintance with the poet, an inwardly warming understanding with each word and each image of these dramas, so that their ever repeated reading of these dramas could count as wandering among the ghostly figures of beloved dead ones, as the continued exchange of the most certain and deepest memories. They felt, however, that this intercourse with the "book" in the hand was only an artificial, indeed unnatural, mediated intercourse with shadows that must pale ashamed before the dramatic reality of the stage. 9[42]

In the pages that follow, this relationship between the modern spectator and the drama is described as a moral relationship—yet this moral theme may already be recognized here, if we remember a passage mentioned earlier (9[105]). There, morality was linked to the "illusory world of representation" and with "the destruction of the originary pain and the originary contradiction." "Everything *good* comes out of the temporary *submersion in representation*, that is out of becoming one with appearance" 9[105]. It is precisely this becoming one with appearance that the "better educated spectators" attempt in reading Shakespeare's "Hamlet." The example that Nietzsche chooses is certainly not insignificant. These readers "with the 'book' in the

hand" feel they have come to an "understanding with each word and
each image" so that reading is like "wandering among the ghostly
figures of beloved dead ones." There is no doubt that the reader
identifies himself here with Hamlet, who, in Act I, scenes iv and v,
wanders with the ghost of his beloved dead father, and who, in Act II,
scene ii, holds a conversation with Polonius—with a book in his hand.
But the attempt to become one with the appearance of *Hamlet* proves
highly problematical, since this text repeatedly indicates and emphasizes the differentiation, the nonadequate nature of the text itself.[19] And things hardly go better for the reader in the actual presence of the dramatic production than they did in his "intercourse with
the book in the hand" 9[42]

> It doesn't work. For even in the mouth of the inwardly most convincing
> actors, we hear a pensive thought, an image, basically each word sounds
> softened down, atrophied, profaned. We don't believe in this language,
> we don't believe in these people and that which otherwise moved us as
> the deepest world revelation is now an unwilling game of masks. And so
> we turn back to the book and confess that the unnatural mediation of the
> printed word seems more natural than the mediation of the spoken word
> in the action as it appears to our senses. But if we now try ourselves to
> read that which we read in silent emotion, to read it aloud with mimetic
> differentiation of the voice, we become once again perplexed that our
> own delivery—in contrast with that emotion, appears totally non-
> adequate—indeed unworthy. 9[42]

With each repetition of the text, in the silent reading, in the stage
realization, in the reading aloud with a mimetic differentiation, the
text shows itself as thought or image, as mediated and nonadequate.
This difference can be eliminated only by means of a pathetic
monotone recitation.

> ... so that we flee now to a general pathetic monotone recitation,
> through which, we at least feel that we have done enough for our exhal-
> tation. 9[42]

A little further on Nietzsche attempts to explain this pathetic
monotone sound.

> What is this, in reality, very unnatural pathos, which is not at all reflected
> in nature? It is the expression of a *moral* state—the opposition of the
> aesthetic world to our own reality comes to us immediately and most
> strongly as a moral feeling, as a feeling of the aesthetic unnaturalness of
> our world in comparison with the nature of the artistic world, indeed as a
> feeling of our unaesthetic, thoroughly moral essence. 9[42]

A double displacement has taken place here. The pathos of the monotone is at first described as an opposition—opposition of the aesthetic world to our own reality—then as a comparison, comparison of the nature of the aesthetic world to our unnaturalness, and in the last description of moral feeling all difference is eliminated. We have simply the feeling of our moral essence.

Morality is becoming one with appearance, the attempt to produce a mimesis that is pure identity. In the birth of tragedy out of music (as we have read in passages 104, 105), appearance (*der Schein*) takes place only through a violent differentiation of the will. Yet the pathetic monotone sound of morality represses this original contradiction, that which is nonadequate.

> The meaning of *beat* as a limitation of music—against its [music's] greatest effect. In the case of Wagner one now and then experiences how music works without it. . . . Beat totally lacks any model in nature: what kind of a power would that be which cut up the impulses of the will with equal time segments?—that is, originally beat is a reflection of the breaking of the waves. It is already a simile of the will—something external. . . . Through the beat, harmony and melody are, as it were, restrained. Beat is the repercussion of *mimesis* on music. 9[116]

Beat must be identified here with the monotone—since beat is "totally without a model in nature," just as the monotone was "not at all reflected in nature" 9[42]. Beat, like the monotone, tries to control the differentiation of the will by cutting up its impulses into equal time segments and by trying to repeat the same thing over and over. Beat has no model in nature (nature in the sense of will), because the will first expresses beat as a simile. The German term *"Gleichnisrede"* suggests not only a simile but also a parable, emphasizing not only the mimetic nature of beat but its moral nature as well.[20]

Nothing stands in greater contrast to this symmetrical, moral beat than the differentiation of mimetic pathos in Wagner.

> The music itself, which becomes forced into the visual scheme, must now be free of all strict forms, that is, above all free of strictly symmetrical rhythm. For dramatic mimesis is something much too changeable, irrational for all forms of absolute music: it can't even hold the beat—and therefore Wagnerian music has the greatest shifts of tempo. This music is grasped once again as produced, *originary music,* because it is limitless: it corresponds to alliteration. 9[149]

Wagner's music, with the greatest shifts in tempo, corresponds to alliteration. This newly introduced, corresponding element (cf. p.

13–14 of this essay), alliteration, will bring us to a much more fruitful element. Alliteration is, of course, a repetition, but a defective one: like Wagner's mimetic pathos, it "can't even hold the beat," a defective repetition, not only because shifts of tempo take place but also since only a part of the previous word is repeated, a fragmentary repetition, therefore, which has nothing to do with a meaningful content. This imitation is so imperfect that the second word in no way gives access to the original word it so partially repeats.

Alliteration brings us to the notion of stammering: the relationship is clear and we can add it without hesitation to the list of corresponding elements of fragment 9[149]. For stammering is defined in Grimm's *German Dictionary*[21] as follows: "conceptually it comes from the striking of the tongue while speaking, through which a more or less frequent [therefore with shifts of tempo like alliteration] repetition of letters and syllables in the words to be articulated is brought about." Yet stammering does distinguish itself somewhat from alliteration. Like alliteration, it is indeed a fragmentary repetition, but a repetition in which an uncontrollably convulsive element comes into play. The etymological meaning of the word "stammer" (in the *Duden Etymological Dictionary*) is "to knock against, to be obstructed": this is detailed through the word's relationship with "dumb, silent"—to be inhibited in speech, incapable of speaking.[22]

This incapability of speaking, this repetition as contradiction, permeates the entire text. For stammering plays both the role of the central metaphor as well as that of metaphor of decentralization. To be sure, the word itself appears in the ninth notebook only twice and one single time in the 1872 *The Birth of Tragedy*; but we are usually unaware of its operation, because its numerous repetitions are so disguised.

The two instances of the term "stammer" in the ninth notebook allow us to enter it into our history. On the one hand, Nietzsche would have us believe that it is a congenital defect of modern man exclusively.

> To this extent Schiller's Song to Joy first gets its deep, true, artistic background. We see how the poet tries to interpret his deep Germanic Dionysian drive in images—how he, however, as modern man, only knows to stammer clumsily. 9[10]

But we can find a more developed explanation of the phenomenon already in the Renaissance, in the case of Hamlet, one of Nietzsche's models.

The thought of the tragic hero must be totally contained in the tragic illusion: he must not want to explain the tragic to us. Hamlet is a model: he always expresses the false thing, always seeks false reasons—tragic knowledge does not enter into his reflection. He has *looked at* the tragic world but he doesn't speak of it, but rather about his weaknesses in which he releases the impression of that view.

The thinking and reflecting of the hero is not Apollonian *insight* into his true essence, but rather an illusionary stammering: the hero errs. 9[28]

Stammering, therefore, although it thrives on words and thought, on the Socratic, misleads the language of science. "The dialectic errs. The language of the dramatic hero is a continual erring, a self-deception" 9[28].

And stammering can be traced even further back in time: it can already be noted in Greek tragedy:

How should the hero now speak? Who is after all—a vision? In Aeschylus he is silent: then he speaks colossal words. 9[7]

The long *silence* of the Aeschylian figures reminds one of the vision of the chorus. . . . Then, such long-silent people had to say terribly pathetic words: they were pushed out too high into the ideal sphere: it must have been totally foreign, uncanny, incomprehensible words. 9[110][23]

Stammering, therefore, has no limits. It appears in every epoch and threatens with a certain breakdown in speech. From the very first, it was never a question of anything else in this essay. For according to the passage just cited, stuttering breaks out in the trajectory between the vision of the chorus and the improvisation of character. And now we are practically back at the starting point of our text, at the birth of tragedy out of music—and we certainly don't want to repeat the whole thing again—only perhaps to indicate briefly how history, the appearance of the interpreting image and stammering all correspond to one another.

What does stammering signify in the trajectory between the Dionysian chorus and the Apollonian image? The strange rule of stammering determines the relationship between the two aesthetic principles. This relationship seemed at first to make possible the articulation between two historical epochs and the temporal succession of the different periods, and, in addition, to guarantee a clear separation between the mimetic, interpreting, image and that which it signifies. The stammer now menaces the definitive distinction between identity and discrepancy, between repetition and contradiction, distinctions without which the concepts of history, signifier and signification are meaningless.

The historical gesture of Nietzsche is Socratic, a gesture which seems to secure the meaning of the text. In this way, its "true goal is camouflaged by a delusion" (*The Birth of Tragedy,* I:31). "The [historical] myth protects us from the [movement of continual reversal]. . . , while at the same time giving it the fullest liberty" (*The Birth of Tragedy,* I: 115).

These fragments, therefore, describe not only the history of tragedy but also the tragedy of history. In this tragedy, the Apollonian, historical Socrates or the historical possibility itself[24] plays the main role—as hero. His world of scientific appearance is driven to its limits where it denies itself.[25] Yet this denial of the Apollonian can hardly accomplish its definitive destruction: what takes place is rather its new entanglement with the Dionysian in the unrelenting game of inversions.

In no way, then, can the frenzy and convulsiveness be contained in an original Dionysian period, for all of history is one single convulsion, the birth pangs of a chain of reproductions in which each descendant may be recognized by one single birth mark—a congenital defect, the stammer. Nietzsche himself does not deny his own problematical inscription into this story, for in the ninth notebook, it is repeatedly a question of his own incapability of speaking.

If we were to draw from his text the appropriate conclusions about our own possibility of interpretation, we would find ourselves confronted with a certain impediment.

RILKE

The Tenth *Duino Elegy* or the
Parable of the Beheaded Reader

CHAPTER TWO

Once upon a time in some remote corner of the universe, diffused in countless glittering solar-systems, there was a star on which clever animals invented knowledge. . . . After a few breaths of nature, the star congealed and the clever animals had to die. One could invent a story in this way and still not have sufficiently illustrated how wretched, shadowy, transient, pointless, and arbitrary the human intellect appears within Nature. (Nietzsche, "Of Truth and Lies in an Extra-moral Sense.")

Wie sie doch alle
wohnen im warmen Gedicht, häuslich, und lang
bleiben im schmalen Vergleich. Teilnehmende.
("An Hölderlin," II: 93)[1]

The clearly marked threshold that opens the last of Rilke's *Duino Elegies*—the interstice between two contradictory modes of language, violent insight on the one side and jubliatory assent on the other—has made this poem readily accessible to a particular line of interpretation.

> Daß ich dereinst, an dem Ausgang der grimmigen Einsicht,
> Jubel und Ruhm aufsinge zustimmenden Engeln. (lines 1–2)

The prefatory passage (lines 1-15) not only predicts the rest of the elegy, the path from the City of Suffering to the celebration of the Realm of Lamentation, but also dictates those texts that have appeared as its commentary.

How they all
live in the warm poem, domestically, and long
remain in the narrow simile. Those who take part.

That I some day, at the exit out of the violent insight,
Might sing jubilation and praise to assenting Angels.

25

That paraphrase should form the basis or ground for most of these commentaries[2] is neither insignificant nor extrinsic to the poem itself. The call in the tenth elegy to praise and assent, to the possibility of affirmation through repetition in language, finds its critical analogon in the paraphrase, an assenting re-presentation of the poetical statement. Little wonder then that such criticism feels itself so at home in this elegy, a text moreover, that promises precisely the recompense of genuine home in return for the acceptance of suffering, for assent/paraphrase:

> Wir, Vergeuder der Schmerzen.
> Wie wir sie absehn voraus, in die traurige Dauer,
> ob sie nicht enden veilleicht. Sie aber sind ja
> unser winterwähriges Laub, unser dunkeles Sinngrün,
> *eine* der Zeiten des heimlichen Jahres—; nicht nur
> Zeit—, sind Stelle, Siedelung, Lager, Boden, Wohnort. (lines 10–15)

The heading of the elegy prescribes the necessity of assenting paraphrase which the main body of the text (lines 16–105) faithfully executes—most clearly through a mythological account of this celebrating assent, but also, as the etymological roots of paraphrase indicate (paraphrazein—to point out alongside) by way of a descriptional rhetoric that passes alongside and points out the sights of the City of Suffering and Realm of Lamentation. The critical essays[3] then become the paraphrase of a paraphrase and we in turn must retrace their itinerary. We must trace this, perhaps indescribable, outline because the poem presents such linearity as the only unambiguous alternative. And the assurance that the literary text will function as an easily accessible "ground" and "home" for its commentary, as a fertile, comfortable earth for its own flourishing, is essential to every critical discourse—even our own.

True to the model presented by the opening line, the main part of the poem begins with the "violent insight" generated by the City of Suffering. A constellation of moral accusations underlies the description of the city's emptied center (lines 16–22), a constellation com-

---

We, squanderers of sorrows.
How we see to the end of them in advance, in the mournful
    duration,
if they are not ending perhaps. They, however, are
our winter foliage, our dark evergreen,
one of the seasons of the secret year—, not only
season—, are place, settlement, storehouse, ground, home.

posed of threats to comprehensibility and truth (falsity, noise, emptiness, violence). The elegy turns then to the vulgar revelry of a nearby
fair (lines 23–38). The fairgrounds are located at the edge of the city
so that, despite the insistence here on chaotic and dizzying fall, the
text has made its first step in the linear ascent toward the mountains
of the Realm of Lamentation. This certainty of progression seems to
determine the topography of the rest of the poem, a topography
layed out as a progressive marking of borders.

Beyond the fair lies the cause for true jubilation and praise promised in the opening lines. In the Realm of Lamentation, all falsity and
violence have apparently been overcome. A highly organized structure of ascending movement replaces the uncontrollable confusion of
the City of Suffering. The oldest lamentation guides the newly dead
youth, pointing out first the subterranean mines (lines 55–60), above
these the fields, animals, and ruins of the land (lines 61–67), then the
more spectacular colossal figure of the Sphinx that rises above them,
and even "higher," the constellations—until finally the youth climbs to
the mountains of originary pain.

The last lines—appended to the main body of the elegy—are the
most disconcerting to the attempt at paraphrase, for the poem itself
no longer proceeds by pointing out sights in the landscape, and the
very concept of assenting paraphrase seems to be supplemented and
supplanted by the notion of *Gleichnis*.

The "we" of these final stanzas can be none other than we the
interpreters. We can trace the text along a ground-of-assent as prescribed by the opening lines of the elegy, producing a faithful outline
that scrupulously avoids doing violence to the poetical text. It is, however, precipitous to accept the innocence of this pre-text for interpretation. Despite the guise of sympathy and gentleness in these verses
("would feel," "sympathy," "almost,") they set the scene for a violent
paradox in which we ourselves are inscribed.

> Und wir, die an *steigendes* Glück
> denken, empfänden die Rührung,
> die uns beinah bestürtzt,
> wenn ein Glückliches *fällt*. (lines 110–13)

> And we who think of *climbing* happiness
> would feel the sympathy,
> that almost staggers us,
> when a happy thing *falls*.

The paraphrastic commentary, pondering the ascending happiness of
the dead, would feel the emotion which "almost staggers"—the emotion that takes place when success or happiness falls. In a four line
passage that italicizes the words "climbing" and "falls," it is impossible
to muffle the syllable *stürzt.* This hurling (*Stürzen*) from the secure,
homelike heights that a reading of the elegy seemed to assure, although well camouflaged, undoubtedly forms the poem's commentary on our attempts at paraphrase.

After this staggering paradox into which paraphrase leads, we have
no choice but to retrace our steps to the origin of the difficulty. The
opening lines called explicitly for a movement away from violent insight toward jubilation and assent, and implicitly for a commentary of
paraphrase. Such a movement seemed unmistakably to take place in
the passage from the City of Suffering to the land of lamentations,
where the older guide speaks unwaveringly as the figure of celebrating assent. Can it be that a more detailed paraphrase would trip itself
up?

The entire elegy pivots around the relationship between the city
and the Realm of Lamentations, and the narration organizes its two
descriptions according to a system of contraries. The difference between the two realms is as pronounced as that between life and
death,[4] and the progression of the elegy depends on that absolute line
of demarcation separating the two. The scission is radical and the
youth who first follows a young lamentation prefers, on good
grounds, to double back. The Realm of Lamentation may only be
entered by the dead.

> Aber er läßt sie, kehrt um,
> wendet sich, winkt . . . Was solls? Sie ist
> eine Klage.

> Nur die jungen Toten, im ersten Zustand
> zeitlosen Gleichmuts, dem der Entwöhnung,
> folgen ihr liebend. (lines 45–49)

Death is systematically repressed in the city, its absolute finality repeatedly written off by "Deathless" beer, the market of consolation

---

But he leaves her, goes back,
turns round, nods . . . What for? She is a complaint.

Only the young dead, in the first state
of timeless equanimity, that of weaning,
follow her lovingly.

and the ready-bought church. The lamentations, on the other hand, give their total assent to death: here the graves and gravestones figure as prized monuments, and their land is that which welcomes the newly dead.

The acquiescence to death is marked by a material refusal of all immediate contact with life, a weaning from the things of this world (*Entwöhnung*). The speech of the older complaint repeatedly points to this absence, the loss of mining riches, once theirs, the ruins where castles and temples once stood, the tombs of a once thriving race. This abstinence from all production and consumption is paralleled in the city by an excess of productivity and exchange beyond all control and an insatiable drive toward immediate satisfaction.

Renunciation governs the Realm of Lamentation as absolutely as another set of commercial notions governs the city—for it too works as a system of exchange. This pattern of abnegation is familiar within a Christian context and also within a certain idealist interpretation of postsymbolist tendencies. At the price of renunciation, the possession of truth has been bought. The wealth of meaning, of full language (for lamentation is above all a form of language) comes with relinquishing the claim to the object that language names. Truth is guaranteed beyond the border of the City of Suffering: just beyond the false promises of the advertisements for "Deathless," it is "real" (line 38). The voice of the older lamentation shows (*zeigt*, lines 50, 62, 64, 67) and names (*nennen*, lines 89, 91, 100), a naming investing everything with rich meaning: the City of Suffering raises up in contrast only an inarticulate din.

One image of the City of Suffering tacked on to the end of its description summarizes its attributes: it repeats them and yet generates them, marking all that remains absent in the Realm of Lamentations. The genitals of money that propagate and promise to stimulate fertility symbolize the vulgar desires, the excessive and meaningless reproduction of the city. In the land of lamentations, no signs of reproduction are to be seen. The distant fathers are chastely referred to at the beginning of the tour and the mothers suggested at the end only by the shining constellation " 'M' which signifies the mothers." Desireless equanimity (*Gleichmut,* line 48), a balance later thematized by the scales, the Pschent crown, the doubled sheet and the cradle, reigns in the Realm of Lamentation.

This outline according to polarities that we have sketched gives us a balanced if somewhat banal picture of the elegy. It was certainly

another paraphrase and we have as yet to locate the error that makes
paraphrase so precarious an enterprise. We have some indication
from the fourth elegy, however, that we are on the right track.

> Da wird für eines Augenblickes Zeichnung
> ein Grund von Gegenteil bereitet, mühsam,
> daß wir sie sähen. (lines 14–16)

The tenth elegy is, to be sure, based on this ground of contradiction:
to say what this means (or cannot mean) is perhaps the only task of
our reading.

If nothing else, this sketch of contrasting values makes evident the
alliance between paraphrase and lamentation. The renunciation of
immediate possession in exchange for a language of truth, this restrained and well-balanced one-to-one economic transaction,[5] this
nonviolent means of reproduction is both that of lamentation and that
of paraphrase, the latter wishing no power over its object other than
to duplicate its significance. The very possibility of organizing the text
around a fixed axis dividing negative and positive values, a reading
which the elegy itself openly calls for, depends on the same assumptions about language as renunciatory naming and paraphrase, the
assumption that a sign may function as a clear and unproblematical
index[6] of a repeatable meaning. Much is at stake then, not only language as truth, the veracity of the poetical voice called forth by the
opening lines of the poem, the powers of the critical text to reproduce
the truth of the poetic text, but also the entire possibility of moral
rectitude assigned to the Realm of Lamentation, in contrast to the
degeneracy of the City of Suffering.

What we have to say now will hardly be staggering: we saw it in
advance at the end of the elegy. It is as though the indiscriminate
proliferation of empty value produced by the genitals of money has
somehow penetrated into the Realm of Lamentation. For another
reading of those very passages where the rhetoric of renunciation is
most literal generates an almost invaginated interpretation:[7] it transforms[8] our paraphrase into paradox.

Is the young lamentation, for example, really a convincing figure of
renunciation? Her welcoming of the newly dead is hardly distinguish-

---

There for the delineation of a moment
a ground of contradiction is prepared, painstakingly,
that we might see it.

able from the mundane gestures of a well-poised adolescent girl. She
walks in coquettish silence with the young men, and with young girls
she is quick to point out her elegant finery, "Pearls of suffering and
the fine / veils of endurance"—patience and suffering capitalized
upon as precious materials. One critic, at least, uncomfortable at this
prospect, has been anxious to ascribe it to her youth.[9] After all, the
dead youth is lead through the Realm of Lamentation by one of the
older and presumably wiser of the race. Yet even the monologue of
the older lamentation does not quite operate as a song of celebration
bound to the acceptance of suffering: the noble reserve of her language barely veils the fact that she quite blatantly laments the loss of
past riches.

> —Wir waren,
> sagt sie, ein Großes Geschlecht, einmal wir Klagen.
>   Die Väter
> trieben den Bergbau dort in dem großen Gebirg;
> . . . .
>   Einst waren wir reich.—
>   (lines 55–56)

She measures the greatness of her race by their former mining
wealth, to be sure a source of value discreetly hidden away, but, nevertheless, the admitted origin of all their former power. The tone of her
commentary, as she points out the ruins of former temples and castles, leaves little doubt as to her nostalgic desires.[10]

As we have noted (note 7), this second reading of the enterprise of
lamentation does not merely sheath the first as its negation, bringing
about the replacement of renunciation by desire: already within the
restrained economy which exchanged renunciation for truth, the desire to draw profit from absence could have been seen.[11] A certain
tonality of irresistible sincerity in the voice of complaint might seem to
belie this rather perverse interpretation: we might, therefore, place
side by side with the tenth elegy another text of Rilke's of equally
irresistible, if somewhat differently articulated, sincerity, "The Letter
of the Young Worker." Its immediate claim to a rapport with the

---

> —We were,
> she says, a great race, once, we complaints. The forefathers
> worked the mine there in the great mountain range;
> . . . .
>   Once we were rich.—

elegy is its date: written between the 12th and 15th of February 1922, the letter was begun the day after and finished within three days of the elegy. The young worker describes renunciation precisely as it functions in the Realm of Lamentation. Unable to conceal an irrepressible material desire, it operates by depreciating the worldly and then borrowing this earthly value in order to displace it and draw profit from it in another realm.

> Sie haben aus dem Christlichen ein métier gemacht, eine bürgerliche Beschäftigung, sur place, einen abwechselnd abgelassenen und wieder angefüllten Teich. Alles, was sie selber tun, ihrer ununterdrückbaren Natur nach (soweit sie noch Lebendige sind), steht im Widerspruch mit dieser merkwürdigen Anlage, und so trüben sie ihr eigenes Gewässer und müssen es immer wieder erneun. Sie lassen sich nicht vor Eifer, das Hiesige... schlect und wertlos zu machen,—und so liefern sie die Erde immer mehr denjenigen aus, die sich bereit finden, aus ihr... wenigstens einen zeitlichen, rasch erspießlichen Vorteil zu ziehn. Diese zunehmende Ausbeutung des Lebens, ist sie nicht eine Folge, der durch die Jahrhunderte fortgesetzten Entwertung des Hiesigen?.... Welcher Betrug, Bilder hiesigen Entzückens zu entwenden, um sie hinter unserm Rücken an den Himmel zu verkaufen! (Volume 6, p. 1114)

To be sure, the young worker disparages specifically a Christian notion of sacrifice. In reading the tenth elegy, one is quick to discount the possibility of the so familiar Christian interpretation in favor of the more distant endeavor of lamentation, investing the latter with a higher value. Yet the reference to the relationship between the City of Suffering and the lamentations soon becomes unmistakable.

> Wird der Tod wirklich durchsichtiger durch diese hinter ihn verschleppten Lichtquellen? Und wird nicht alles hier Fortgenommene, da

---

They have made a métier of that which is Christian, a bourgeois occupation, *sur place*, an alternately drained and filled pool. All that they do themselves, according to their irrepressible nature (in so far as they are still alive), stands in contradiction with this remarkable investment, and so they muddy their own waters and must repeatedly renew them. Out of zeal, they do not refrain from making the earthly ... wicked and worthless,—and thus they deliver the earth more and more to those who find themselves prepared to draw from it at least a transient, rapidly profitable advantage. This growing exploitation of life, is it not the result of the depreciation of the earthly continued over centuries? ... What a deception, to steal images of earthly delight in order to sell them behind our backs to heaven!

Does death really become clearer by means of these light sources dragged behind it? And isn't everything that is taken from here, since after all no vacuum can maintain itself, replaced by a deception,—are the cities therefore filled with so much ugly artificial light and noise because the authentic radiance and song has been delivered over to a Jerusalem to be gained later?

nun doch kein Leeres sich halten kann, durch einen Betrug ersetzt,—
sind die Städte deshalb von so viel häßichem Kunstlicht und Lärm er-
füllt, weil man den echten Glanz und den Gesang an ein später zu be-
ziehendes Jerusalem ausgeliefert hat? (Volume 6, p. 1115)

There will be much to say about the operation of the double deception here described. It operates first as a borrowing of images from
life to sell them to the beyond, and this is necessarily followed by a
second deception, the noisy artificiality of the cities appearing in lieu
of the song delivered elsewhere.

That a certain fraud takes place in the Realm of Lamentation is, in
any case, beyond doubt; the swindle is even subversively suggested by
a word much emphasized by its positioning in the verse—"Nicht erfaßt es sein Blick, im Frühtod / schwindelnd." *Schwindelnd* functions in
all senses of the word; the dead youth staggers dizzily in this realm,
and he is also being swindled by that which his gaze cannot grasp, by
the face or head of the Sphinx.

This staggering swindle answers the riddle of the last lines of the
elegy as to why paraphrase fails: it depended on taking those first
lines of the poem at face value, on jubilantly assenting to the thrust
toward the Realm of Lamentation and on viewing it as a clear progression away from its contrary, the fraudulent City of Suffering.
Unambiguous assent proves impossible in the land of lamentations
and therefore proves impossible in the paraphrastic commentary that
depends on their integrity to win a secure place for itself.

We have hardly progressed, however, in saying what the elegy actually signifies or in clarifying the relationship between the City of Suffering and the lamentations, the principle subject of the entire poem.
The Realm of Lamentation is doubly inscribed in the text, on the one
hand, as the very opposite of the City of Suffering and, on the other,
as the same, leading us to the dizzying conclusion that the two realms
are both absolutely different and alike.

This type of conclusion precludes any fully rational analysis and yet
the elegy leaves us little choice, since every attempt to define this
rapport will repeatedly lead to similar contradictions. The two realms,
for example, are organized by clear if contrary temporal designations.
The City of Suffering figures as our present, modern world, while the
land of lamentations operates as its origin. Its originary nature is
evident from the emphasis on the lamentations as a race of the past
(its images borrowed from ancient Egypt) and from the orientation of
the whole land toward *originary*-suffering (*Ur-leid*). Yet this realm is no

less the land of the dead, the telos of earthly life. That the Realm of
Lamentation should function as both origin and telos need not necessarily mark a contradiction; one could read here instead a certain
complicity with other logo- and theocentric structures already noted
and interpret this as a verification of its hallowed nature. Yet a certain
repetition of this structure takes place in such a way as to shake the
very ground of its theocentricity.

This repetition takes place in language. The lamentations are—
their personification makes one all but forget it—before anything
else language, a language that recapitulates and names the things of
the earth, that transforms the earth (*verwandelt*[12]) into poetry and thus
operates as its telos. The opening lines of the poem give us every
reason to believe that the enterprise of lamentation is totally merged
with this transformation through poetry, and the older complaint
does little else than point out and name. Yet we are thrown off balance when we begin to note that this figure of language has no language of her own: over and over she names in terms of human experience and human language.

> ... bei Menschen
> findest du manchmal ein Stück geschliffenes Ur-Leid
> oder, aus altem Vulkan, schlackig versteinerten
>   Zorn. (lines 57–59)

> (Lebendige kennen sie nur als sanftes Blattwerk) (line 66)

> Langsam nennt sie die Klage:—Hier,
> siehe; den *Reiter,* den *Stab,* und das vollere Sternbild
> nennen sie: *Fruchtkranz.* (lines 89–91)

>   In Ehrfurcht
> nennt sie sie, sagt;—Bei den Menschen
> ist sie ein tragender Strom.—(lines 99–101)

> ... among humans
> you sometimes find a piece of polished originary-suffering
> or, from an old volcano, some slaggy, petrified wrath. (lines 57–59)

> (The living know them only as gentle foliage) (line 66)

> Slowly the complaint names them:—Here,
> see; the *Rider,* the *Staff,* and the more complete constellation
> they call *Fruit Wreath.* (lines 89–91)

>   In reverence
> she names them, says;—among men
> it is a carrying stream.—(lines 91–101)

The very figure that should transform the things of the human earth into language repeatedly calls on human language to name the things of her realm. If lamentation functions as the textual telos of the earth, the earth functions no less as the textual telos of the Realm of Lamentation. It is no longer clear who's naming what or what's being named. This reversibility of roles between the lamentations and the human, as namer and named, as telos and origin, can no longer be written off as a theocentric valorization of the Realm of Lamentation. Quite the contrary: we are getting a glimpse at a dizzying endless displacement of origin and telos that precludes any definitive location of a center.

Certainly, we have not answered the question "What is lamentation?" Yet we here begin to note that this question "What is" proves illogical in the context of a text which, as we have just seen, sends the traditional relationship of signifier and signified into a spin—where the signified proves to be nothing other than another language whose signified, in turn, is another language.

This continual displacement of the literal content of the poetic text has troubled our insight in the somewhat naive attempts at reading made to this point. Nothing could be taken at face value. Each clearly marked guideline that the elegy presents proves a dizzying deception— making an outline of the whole indescribable. The call to assent/ascent/ paraphrase led to paradox and fall; the organization of the poem according to polar opposites—the single organization that seemed to make sense—showed the Realm of Lamentations to be not only the contrary of the City of Suffering but also its image.

The elegy itself, foreseeing our stunned perplexity at the end of the main body of the text, offers to awaken us from our dazed state by raising up a *Gleichnis*:

> Aber erweckten sie uns, die unendlich Toten, ein Gleichnis,
> siehe, sie zeigten vielleicht auf die Kätzchen der leeren
> Hasel, die hängenden, oder
> meinten den Regen, der fällt auf dunkles Erdreich im
> Frühjahr.—(lines 106–09)

But if they awakened for us, the endlessly dead, an
    image [*Gleichnis*],
look, they would point perhaps to the catkins of the empty
hazel, the hanging ones, or
they would mean the rain that falls on dark earth in
    the spring.—

To be sure, the images of the catkins and the rain hardly provide the unambiguous explanation of the elegy's contradictions. Yet this may be the single point where it will be fruitful to take the text at its word[13] and to assume that the *Gleichnis* (and not only the specific one given) will be able to give us a picture of what has happened. Yet the *Gleichnis* that the dead might awaken for us is certainly no traditional image for the implied similarity between catkins and rain on the one hand and the "unendingly dead" on the other is not immediately apparent. One would tend to say rather that the text *redet in Gleichnissen*—it speaks in riddles, and not only here but throughout the elegy, riddles that pivot around the endless significance of the *Gleichnis*.

A reading of the poem as unproblematical image (*Gleichnis*) and the assumption that the critical text, in turn, could re-present through its paraphrastic imagery (*Gleichnis*) the content of the first text, leads to the paradoxical and violent riddle (*Gleichnis*) of the last lines. The elegy itself relates a moral parable (*Gleichnis*), the rejection of the false jubilation of the City of Suffering in exchange for the true celebration and assent in the Realm of Lamentation: this moral virtue is subverted, however, through the very gesture of renunciation which claims access to the truth, a renunciation that functions rather as a swindle. We are able at least to venture saying that the *Gleichnis* that can definitively explain our predicament is neither the representative image nor the moral parable, although both of these play a part in the scenario. Yet to say what this *Gleichnis* seems to designate—violent paradox or deceptive fraud—only begins to unmask its nature.

How then is one to understand this paradox and swindle? And will the gesture that attempts to do so write off the possibility of comprehension? If we reconsider the relationship between the City of Suffering and the Realm of Lamentation, we begin to see that it is nothing other than that of a *Gleichnis*. This relationship between the two realms was seen to operate first as contrast, a comparison (*Gleichnis*) of opposition, and then as a relationship of similarity in which each functioned as the image (*Gleichnis*) of the other. If we retrace the change of this relation between the two poles of this *Gleichnis*, we can note some of the radical difficulties.

It was precisely through the initial contrast between the two realms that the elegy presented a clear contour of sense—both meaning and direction—a sense that was announced in the opening lines by the image of a definitive threshold of separation between violence and assent, a radical scission echoed in the body of the text between evil and good, between falseness and truth, between falling and ascent, between the human and the image. But when the morally elevated complaints also functioned as swindlers, when their truth proved to be falsity as well, when the ascent of the dead youth was marred by dizziness, when the image turned out to be no less imag*ed*, a new relationship of *Gleichnis*, similarity rather than contrasting comparison, entered the scene in such a way as to totally undermine the very controlled generation of sense determined by the original structure of unidirectional movement through a threshold. The main body of the poem operates then as a *Gleichnis*—

1) As a parable, but one in which the moral absolutes are thoroughly undermined.

2) Unmistakably as image, but the whole then taking on the structure of a sign whose signifier and signified are apparently interchangeable, and whose ability to make sense is therefore totally subverted.

3) As a comparison which defines its elements by aligning them as polar opposites, a comparison which, through a complex doubling (invagination) of the Realm of Lamentation, also aligns them as analogous.

Although we have hardly begun to weigh the rich possibilities of the *Gleichnis,* it is already evident that this kind of speculation writes off the possibility of the clear insight it seemed to promise. Perhaps we have interpreted the *Gleichnis* as too indiscriminately sown throughout the text, especially since the last lines of the poem seem to place specific limitations on it, "Aber erweckten sie uns, die unendlich Toten, ein Gleichnis." Whatever the following lines may signify, they are presented as an image of those dead whom we have seen to pass through the Realm of Lamentation, and it is in this passage that we will have to seek a further explication of the *Gleichnis.* Certainly no part of the poem's lengthy descriptions justifies being designated as the unique source of the enigmatic comparison to catkins and rain, yet the encounter of the dead youth with the Sphinx, during which a bird retraces the outline of his face, thematizes remarkably our present predicament, that of the *Gleichnis* as riddle (of the Sphinx) on the one hand and as portrait or image on the other.

Nicht erfaßt es sein Blick, im Frühtod
schwindelnd. Aber ihr Schaun,

hinter dem Pschent–Rand hervor, scheucht es die Eule. Und sie,
streifend im langsamen Abstrich die Wange entlang,
jene der reifesten Rundung,
zeichnet weich in das neue
Totengehör, über ein doppelt
aufgeschlagenes Blatt, den unbeschreiblichen Umriß (lines 80–87)

In this cryptical passage—apparently presenting nothing more than
an equilibrium in which Sphinx and spectator face one another, the
overwhelming stillness makes it difficult to grasp (much less to say)
just what takes place. If we are to take the text at its word—an "indescribable outline" takes its place in the incomprehensible space of a
"doubly opened up sheet."

There is much evidence for the radical nature of this enigmatic
inscription. The accompanying lamentation is abruptly cut short in
her role as guide. She "leads" the dead youth through the landscape
(line 161), "shows" him the columns (line 62), "shows" him the tear-
trees (lines 64f.), "shows" him the animals (line 67), and "leads" him to
the graves of the ancestors (line 70). Yet after these excessively re-
dundant reminders of the lamentation's total control, the Sphinx
breaks in upon the scene through no guiding or pointing out of her
own.

> . . . und bald
> mondets empor, das über Alles
> wachende Grab-Mal. (lines 72–74)

Throughout the scene that follows, the only posture the lamentation
will assume is that of passive astonishment (line 77).

The Sphinx thus immediately signals the silencing of the apparently unproblematical voice of paraphrase (that passes alongside and
points) and with it of all that we have seen the power of that voice to

---

His glance does not grasp it, in early death
staggering/swindling. But their looking,
out from behind the pschent, it frightens the owl. And it,
in a slow downstroke, grazing along the cheek,
the one with the ripest roundness,
delineates softly in the new
hearing of the dead, over a doubly
opened up sheet, the indescribable outline.

> . . . and soon
> it rises up like the moon, the all
> watching grave-monument.

imply—the access to truth through language. The Sphinx usurps the head position of the lamentation: "the exhalted Sphinx" with the "crownly head." We must not interpret this usurpation too precipitously as a simple transfer of mastery, nor as another expression of the originary forces of the Realm of Lamentation (implied by the emphasis on ancestral origin and originary pain). This archeo-logical figure of the sphinx is neither a new *arché* (origin) nor is it logical—but rather the violent if camouflaged disintegration of these possibilities.

> Und sie staunen dem krönlichen Haupt, das für immer,
> schweigend, der Menschen Gesicht
> auf die Waage der Sterne gelegt. (lines 77–79)

The Sphinx not only silences the voice of paraphrase, it places the human *Gesicht* on the scale of the stars. This placing on the scale involves great risks,[14] for the *Gesicht* which is being weighed is both the human countenance and the ability to see (in the full sense of the word)—what will be seen to be the weighing of the possibility of weighing, judging, and philosophizing. The measuring of the face/sight that places it in the stars brings about nothing less than a beheading and blinding that is the loss of human reason and (in)sight, the loss of the human itself. This blinding is spelled out quite literally by the text. The glance of the dead youth cannot grasp the overwhelming face of the Sphinx: "His glance does not grasp it, in early death / staggering." Rendered incapable of understanding, he has indeed lost his head in a figural sense. This loss of the power to comprehend is emphasized by the sketching of a drawing into his hearing (*Totengehör*) where the written cannot possibly be perceived.

The more literal references to decapitation are better camouflaged. It is described first by the placing of the human face on a scale, clearly a measuring of the human head by and against the head of the Sphinx (lines 77–79). The human face is placed there by the owl that traces the cheek of the dead youth and inscribes his image in the stars. These lines are not unlike the very last of the elegy—governed by a carefully articulated tonality of mildness in which a certain violence threatens to break loose. The movement that effects this violence is difficult to follow; the text implies it to be indescribable—it is certainly not logi-

---

And they are astonished at the crownly head, that, forever,
silently, has placed the human face
on the scale of the stars.

cal. This concealed execution can however be traced here and there in the passage.

Each word that conveys the sense of faithful tracing and gentle writing—*streifend, Abstrich, zeichnet, Umriß*—is subtly double-edged, for each plays also upon the possibilities of cutting and destruction. *Streifen* indicates not only the grazing of the cheek but also a "striking off" and serves, for example, also to mean the skinning of an animal. The *Abstrich* of the owl is, of course, a downstroke, as in writing, but the noun comes from the verb *Abstreichen,* which signifies a scraping off, a striking out, a canceling from books and even the whetting of a sharp blade. In a conventional context, the verb *Zeichnen* would also function innocently, yet the elegy forces it into a strangely active role—"*zeichnet weich in das neue / Totengehör*"—as though the outline were branded or engraved into the new hearing. *Umriß*, like *Abstrich*, echoes the violence of its verbal form, *umreißen*, which means not only to sketch but also to tear down.

One need only glance at Rilke's early works to verify that such themes are by no means solely the product of a violence done to the text by a forced interpretation.[15] The most striking example is the short story "Frau Blaha's Maid," that ends in a gruesome scene of decapitation. The deranged country girl, Anuschka, brought to the city as a maid, no sooner gives birth to an illegitimate child than she strangles it with an apron sash and stores the corpse in her trunk. Soon afterward, she buys herself a puppet theater and delights the neighborhood children with her presentations, while always promising to bring forth the *ganz große* puppet. As she one day returns to the kitchen carrying the long dead baby, she finds the children have fled in anticipation of the horrible event.

> Sie lachte leise und stieß das Theater mit den Füßen um und trat die einzelnen dünnen Brettchen, welche doch den Garten bedeuteten, entzwei. Und dann, als die Küche schon ganz dunkel war, ging sie herum und spaltete allen Puppen die Köpfe, auch der großen blauen. (Volume 4, p. 629)

It is the fourth elegy that will later play specifically on the image of

---

She laughed softly and kicked over the theater and trampled into pieces the individual thin boards that had represented the garden. And then, when the kitchen was already completely dark, she went around and split the heads of all the puppets, also that of the large blue one.

the puppet theater, and the last lines of that text verify rather explicitly that the particular scene we find in the tenth, the inscription of the dead youth into the constellations, also entails such a deadly violence. In the earlier elegy, the displacement of the child into the stars is complete death even before life.

> Wer zeigt ein Kind, so wie es steht? Wer stellt
> es ins Gestirn und giebt das Maß des Abstands
> ihm in die Hand? Wer macht den Kindertod
> aus grauem Brot, das hart wird,—oder läßt
> ihn drin im runden Mund, so wie den Gröps
> von einem schönen Apfel?...... Mörder sind
> leicht einzusehen. Aber dies: den Tod,
> den ganzen Tod, noch *vor* dem Leben so
> sanft zu enthalten und nicht bös zu sein,
> ist unbeschreiblich. (lines 76–85, Fourth *Duino Elegy*)

As in the last elegy, the violence is marked and camouflaged by mildness (it is *sanft*) and the paradoxical inscription, as in the tenth, is called *unbeschreiblich*. It is indescribable not only because the center of reason has been cut off but also because the motivation for murder cannot be reduced to the moral opposite of good ("and not be evil").

This verification of the violence in the tenth elegy raises more problems than it solves. Why is the violence quite literally marked down and concealed by gentleness? How does this first paradox relate to the impossibility of distinguishing moral absolutes of good and evil (an impossibility we have already witnessed in the case of the tenth elegy)? What can the beheading of an already dead man possibly signify? How is one to link these problems with the loss of reason and sense and the producing of a sign or portrait (*Gleichnis*) that cannot be described?

Who shows a child just as it stands? Who places
it in the stars and gives it the measure of difference
in its hand? Who makes the child-death
of gray bread, that becomes hard,—or leaves
it there in the round mouth, like the core
of a beautiful apple?...... Murderers are
easy to comprehend. But this—so
gently to contain death, the entire death,
even *before* life, and not be evil
is indescribable.

At the risk of adding to this dizzying line of questioning, we might try to grasp the meaning of the figure of the Sphinx. It was, after all, somewhat unnecessary to turn to "Frau Blaha's Maid" and the fourth elegy to prove than an execution takes place in the presence of the Sphinx. The name Sphinx means "throttler"[16] and the mythological monster, that the elegy insists on linking to its own image (it is "brotherly to the one on the Nile"), in fact, throttled and devoured those who dared face her.

Strangely enough, it is only the face or the head of the Sphinx that we encounter in the elegy.[17] The appositional description of the term "Sphinx" reads: "the exhalted Sphinx-; countenance of the silenced chamber:" and when the dead youth and the lamentation are astonished by the Sphinx, "they are astonished at the crownly *head*" (italics mine). Perhaps this explains the possibility of interpreting the figure as a benign object of admiration which, bearing a human face, has raised it to lofty heavenly heights.[18] But the face covers a concealed cavity or chamber that it eclipses,[19] and what is it that the Sphinx countenance camouflages if not that part of its body that, behind the human head, is the nonhuman or monstrous nature of the figure that renders it deadly. The severed head is articulated onto the rest of the monster so as to make its appearance harmless. This articulation works as the gentle lure of apparent sublimity, but also as the fatal trap, for it signals that decapitation in face of the Sphinx has been carried out even before the arrival of the dead youth. The text speaks of this executionary displacement of the human head onto the scale as already having taken place.

> Und sie staunen dem krönlichen Haupt, das *für immer,*
> schweigend, der Menschen Gesicht
> auf die Waage der Sterne gelegt. (lines 77–79—italics mine)

As illogical as it may seem that the dead youth is both already executed and to be executed, the text takes special pains to insist that the head that is transferred to the monster is specifically that of the dead youth. The noun "Sphinx" which is mythologically and lexicographically feminine (*die Sphinx*) appears in the elegy as "der Sphinx"— "*brotherly* to the one on the Nile" (italics mine).

And they are astonished at the crownly head, that, forever,
silently, has placed the human face
on the scale of the stars.

We can now begin to delineate the pattern of the *Schwindel* that first appeared in relation to the lamentations. Certainly a deception is taking place here and the verbal adjective *schwindelnd* may just as well suggest an act of the Sphinx as loss of consciousness in the dead youth.

> Und sie staunen dem krönlichen Haupt ...
> ....
> Nicht erfaßt es sein Blick, im Frühtod
> schwindelnd. (lines 77–81)

This swindle of the Sphinx parallels rather faithfully (with a macabre twist) the double deception that the young worker describes in "The Letter of the Young Worker." In the letter, images of the human realm were sold secretly to the heavens, and to complete the double deception, a new fraud filled the emptiness to replace that which was taken away (Volume 6, pp. 1114–15, cited p. 32 of this essay). Something similar takes place in face of the Sphinx. The countenance of the dead youth had already been displaced to the monstrous body of the sublime and heavenly Sphinx, and a deceptive, if silent, double seems to have replaced the severed head.

The most revealing clue to the understanding of this deception and its radical consequences lies in a text which is all but present and yet camouflaged, camouflaged not only by the elegy but also by a certain snare in the clue itself. The clue is, of course, nothing other than the riddle.

> ... she now asked every Theban wayfarer a riddle taught her by the Three Muses: "What being, with only one voice, has sometimes two feet, sometimes three, sometimes four, and is weakest when it has the most?" Those who could not solve the riddle she throttled and devoured on the spot.[20]

The riddle functions as a kind of game, but a game which has a sense: at least it presents itself as a question directed toward a particular answer that, in solving the enigma, resolves all contradictions and gives the nonsensical text a logical meaning.[21] The answer to the riddle of the Sphinx is, of course, "Man." Certainly, nothing less drastic is placed in (the) question here.

And they are astonished at the crownly head ...
....
His glance does not grasp it, in early death
staggering/swindling.

If the wayfarer can utter the answer—Man—we can only presume that, like that unique exception Oedipus, he will escape the fate of being throttled—or, in terms of the elegy, that he will not lose his head, his face/sight (*Gesicht*). And when the riddle is solved, the answerer saves not only his own particular head but also the human (head) in general, both the integrity of man (by locating his head as center), as well as the possibility of reason in general. He asserts the unity of that single voice ("a being with one voice") over the contradictory multiplicity of four members, two members, three members. And the assertion of human reason and its unambiguous voice takes place not only in the content of the solution but, as has already been implied, in the act of verbally solving the riddle. Speaking with "one voice" is the ability to speak the truth, to reason out the solution, to say that which is no longer contradictory.

All this seems very promising and reasonable. Yet if it is the Sphinx (and most particularly the Sphinx of the tenth elegy) who sets forth the riddle, the reasonability of the enigma is thoroughly shaken. The Sphinx, who in Rilke's text appears only as face and head, who presents to the onlooker only his human facet, has, by his presence, already given the answer to the riddle. The already solved riddle then is none. And the riddle is rendered senseless not only because the solution to the supposed enigma is already there but also because the very answer, as which the human head of the Sphinx functions, indicates the impossibility of all that a solution implies. The answer "Man" seems to assure his integrity over the disparity of his multiple forms, yet the human head on the shoulders of the Sphinx indicates both the severance of that head from its human body and the assembling of discrepant parts to form the monstrous. This monstrous answer to the riddle, the face of the Sphinx that so stuns the dead youth, rather than asserting the rationality of man, his univocal powers of speech, signals a loss of those powers that has "für immer" taken place, a throttling which has already silenced that voice before it could proffer a word.

The riddle operates than as a contradictory text. It gives the semblance of referring to a reconciliatory solution that renders its contradiction logical, but puts forth that very solution as yet another enigma, one that excludes or suspends the possibility of a meaningful solution.

All this takes place in the elegy through a double inscription of the head of man, once on the shoulders of the dead youth and again on those of the Sphinx, once as a principle of integrity and again as an indication of execution and discrepancy, once as center of the ratio and again as sign of the insoluble enigma and loss of reason, once as confirmation of the univocality that the opening lines of the elegy affirmed and again as either the silencing of that voice or its equivocality.

The tracing of the face of the dead youth was just this double inscription, once as the faithful reproduction, the gently marked outline, and once as the violent severance of that which was being traced—the head, and with it the possibility of a re-production that is affirmation or concurrence; a doubling of the significance of doubling then—first as continuity assuring duplication and second as violent cleavage.

Yet how meaningful is this "first, second" that my own exposition seems to imply? To be sure, it is precisely this doubling or duplicity that has been seen to lie at the very center of the elegy and that we have still to puzzle out—and our repeated strategem has been to move away from the concept of gentle repetition toward a certain violence, perhaps implying a definitive usurpation of the gentleness it replaces. Yet the violence that takes place is more violent than the apparently containable, unidirectional, execution so often described here: there was no other alternative if it was to make sense. The more violent violence lies in the irreducibility of the double inscription that cannot be reduced to a definitive cancellation of life and truth by death and falsity. It operates as a duplicity which never resolves itself, as an always doubled inscription. Therefore, the outline drawn by the owl presents no simple delineatory trace: its doubleness renders it "inde*scribable*"—incapable of being re-presented in writing or figures and incapable of being observed and comprehended. The surface of the inscription, the "doubly opened up sheet" defies the notion of the two-dimensional space of print immediately present to human perception, for the sheet has been twice unfolded, offering two different surfaces for the discrepant inscriptions.

This doubling is, of course, the *Gleichnis,* which I long ago set out to define and which has proved to demand a double definition, once as successful re-production and once as the cutting that has placed the notion of man in question. If we follow this unmanning which also functions as reproduction, we will be able to attempt interpreting the end of the elegy, those last eight lines cut off from the main body of the poem.

One is forced then to take a closer look at the genitals of money,
even though the elegy's chaste tone has warned against this vulgar
curiosity, for here the severed organ, sign of unmanning, as in the
encounter with the Sphinx, is coupled with a strange kind of reproduction.

> ... denn Buden jeglicher Neugier
> werben, trommeln und plärrn. Für Erwachsene aber
> ist noch besonders zu sehn, wie das Geld sich
>   vermehrt, anatomisch,
> nicht zur Belustigung nur: der Geschlechtsteil des Gelds,
> alles, das Ganze, der Vorgang—, das unterrichtet
>   und macht
> fruchtbar........(lines 28–33)

It is perhaps injudicious to take this moral warning so lightly, for by
falling prey to our curiosity, in the hopes of being instructed and
thereby turning our own text into a fruitful production, we, no less
than the dead youth in face of the Sphinx, will be confronted with a
loss of reason and sense, the basis of our own interpretive control. For
despite the announcement that the entire scene will be open to the
understanding and that the copulation may be imitated ("that instructs and makes one / fertile"), the process of reproduction here
described precludes the possibility both of comprehension and repeatability. That which propagates itself is money, certainly a measure
full of value, a representation with a meaning behind it; yet this proliferation gives forth merely the sign of value and the sign becomes,
by the very act that produces it, cut off from its source, from that of
which it is presumably a re-production, from that which gave it meaning. This cutting off is signaled, of course, by the castrated organ of
money that, in turn, bears its progeny "anatomically," by dissection,
by cutting away. The scene plays out the production of signs which,
cut off from their referent, have lost their significance, yet which are
strangely potent enough to continue generating in the same senseless
manner. The restrained economy of renunciation, in which immedi-

---

... for booths for every curiosity
woo, drum, and bawl. For adults, however,
there is still something special to see, how the money
      propagates, anatomically,
not merely for entertainment, the sexual organ of money,
all, the whole thing, the procedure that instructs and makes one
fertile.........

ate gratification is sacrificed for the regulated minting of truth, has given way to that of an uncontrollable proliferation, immeasurable in its pace, and especially in the nature of its product.

The genitals of money operate, on the one hand, as the ultimate image of degeneration, and they may seem to be contained by means of this moral relegation. But they inscribe themselves a second time as the metaphor for the incalculable generation of senseless image (*Gleichnis*)—the image generating image. As in the case of the Sphinx, the threat to reason seems contained by the single inscription, but the severance from reason (the head) and originary source (the phallus) is written in as an ever-potent possibility. This means, of course (we have seen it recur over and over in the elegy), that the poem is the site of its own reproduction. By doubly inscribing the notion of reproduction, it re-produces itself in a manner that castrates the original reference of its text and thus cuts off its own potential to make sense.

We are on the verge then of being fully wakened from the stupor into which the paraphrase originally lulled us, wakened into an understanding (which precludes all understanding) of the *Gleichnis*.

> Aber erweckten sie uns, die unendlich Toten, ein Gleichnis,
> siehe, sie zeigten vielleicht auf die Kätzchen der leeren
> Hasel, die hängenden, oder
> meinten den Regen, der fällt auf dunkles
>   Erdreich im Frühjar.—(lines 106–09)

Were the endlessly dead to awaken for us an image, they would point to the phallic catkins of the hazel,[22] those which, having disseminated their seed, having reproduced, hang impotent, cut open, castrated on the branch. Thus, the parallel image of the fertilizing rain. And lest the violence of these benignly fertilizing images seem exaggerated, one has only to read these lines another time. The dead might point to the *Kätzchen,* which are none other than the cat-like sphinxes—"the hanging ones," those who throttle, behead, and thoroughly block the possibility of clear pointing, or they might mean the rain "der fällt," which not only falls but also fells, cuts down, castrates, beheads.

But if they awakened (for) us, the endlessly dead,
    an image [*Gleichnis*],
look, they would point perhaps to the catkins of the empty
hazel, the hanging ones, or
they would mean the rain that falls on dark earth in
    the spring.

This brings us to our own fall, or being felled that the last lines of
the elegy so gently imply.

Und wir, die an *steigendes* Glück
denken, empfänden die Rührung,
die uns beinah bestürzt,
wenn ein Glückliches *fällt*. (lines 110–13)

We have already suspected that this confounding (*Bestürzen*) was more
precipitous than the sympathetic tone implies. We are prepared now
to see just how precipitous. The "steigendes Glück" which we think of
is, of course, that of the young dead climbing triumphantly into the
mountains of originary-suffering, but it is no less the erection of our
own joyous potency, which, having given forth its ejaculation of
paraphrastic assent, doubles violently back on itself to see that this
happy thing must fall. A short fragment, a single line cut off from any
immediate context, written only six days after the creation of the
elegy, provides the link we are missing.

"Dies ist das schweigende Steigen der Phallen" (Volume 2, p. 473).
The increasing happiness is the silent ascent of phalluses (*Phallen*)—
but (and the play here is unmistakable) it is no less the silenced,
camouflaged mounting of traps (*Falle-n*), which is, of course, the ascendancy of falling (*Fall-en*). *Phallen, Falle-n, Fall-en, Fällen*—we see
here the nature of the Rilkean constellation, the *Sternbild*, the *Bild*, the
Gleichnis, that in the spasm of reproducing itself gelds itself.

Perhaps this interpretation of the climax will enable us to sketch an
integral outline of the elegy. The last strophes are cut off from and
yet linked to the central part of the text by an asterisk—the single star
which, according to Webster,[23] has the double function of either referring to a presence or indicating an absence. It articulates the tail
end of the poem to the main body, the lines that we have seen to
elaborate neither presence nor absence but a complex play between
the two. This phallus, although (and because) cut off, we have seen to
fructify the main body of the text—and it does so in such a way that
the descriptions of the City of Suffering and the Realm of Lamentation underwent an incalculable series of reproductions. We have at
length noted the consequences of this proliferation and must now

---

And we who think of *climbing* happiness
would feel the sympathy,
that almost staggers us,
when a happy thing *falls*.

reorient the relationship of this body to those first lines of the elegy that set us on a straight path and therefore led us astray. This heading of the text that prescribed a faithful execution of its call to assent has, of course, been executed in a second sense of the word.

And what about this main body of the elegy severed from its head and from the source of its seed—how can we delineate its contours? Certainly not as the City of Suffering on the one hand and the Realm of Lamentation, on the other, for each has proved a *Gleichnis* of the other. And the proliferation of *Gleichnisse* was hardly contained there, for throughout the poem we have noted the incalculable reproduction of image on image, that left its contours "indescribable." My own text has itself been nothing more than a *Gleichnis,* a paraphrase, that found itself uncontrollably doubled back on itself in a proliferation of images of images, that tells no other tale than the execution of its own reason.

ARTAUD

The Assimilating Harmony: *Héliogabale*

CHAPTER THREE

INITIATION

*S'il y a autour du cadavre d'Héliogabale, mort
sans tombeau, et égorgé par sa police dans les latrines de son palais, une intense circulation de sang
et d'excréments, il y a autour de son berceau une
intense circulation de sperme. (Initial lines of*
Héliogable, *p. 15)*[1]

*On n'est pas initié d'ailleurs qu'à des opérations, et
à des rites, à des signes extérieurs, à des passes
hiéroglyphiques qui nous mettent sur la voie du
secret. (p. 93)*

Initiation into the "conscious chaos" (*Théâtre*, p. 139) of *Héliogabale or
the Anarchist Crowned* takes place, of necessity, as cruelty—a cruelty
manifest from the very beginning in those concrete referents of its
initial lines—blood, excrement, and sperm—that continue to circulate
throughout the entire text. These, along with other similar excesses—
castration, sacrifice, assassination, parricide, debauchery—so completely
dominate Héliogabale's historical biography that no interpretation
can escape a confrontation with that which Artaud terms "cruelty."
And yet, when Artaud explicitly touches upon this term, in the
"Letters on Cruelty,"[2] he rejects the literal meaning of the word—as
blood or flesh.[3]

Il ne s'agit dans cette Cruauté ni de sadisme ni de sang, du moins pas de
façon exclusive. (*Théâtre*, p. 120)

If, surrounding the cadaver of Héliogabale, dead without a tombstone and butchered
by his police in the latrines of his palace, there is an intense circulation of blood and
excrement, there is surrounding his cradle an intense circulation of sperm. (Initial lines
of *Héliogabale*, p. 15.)

Moreover one is never initiated into anything but operations, rites, exterior signs, and
hieroglyphic passwords that place us on the path [*la voie*] of the secret. (p. 93)

On peut très bien imaginer une cruauté pure, sans déchirement charnel.
(*Théâtre*, p. 121)[4]

Cruauté n'est pas en effet synonyme de sang versé, de chair martyre.
(*Théâtre*, p. 121)

By taking the word in its broad sense, rather, Artaud claims to
effect a decisive break with the meaning of language.

Ce mot de cruauté doit être pris dans un sens large, et non dans le sens
matériel. . . . Et je revendique, ce faisant, le droit de briser avec le sens
usuel du langage, de rompre une bonne fois l'armature, de faire sauter
le carcan, d'en revenir enfin aux origines étymologiques de la langue qui
á travers des concepts abstraits évoquent toujours une notion concrète.
(*Théâtre*, pp. 120f.)

If one reads to the letter, the text promises to return from abstract
concepts to the concrete origins of language ("to the etymological
origins"). Such an interpretation may harmonize with that reading of
The Theater and Its Double that sees Artaud's proposed elimination of
the traditional written text as an attempt to reach a concrete and pure
immediacy.[5] Yet, certainly, taking the text at its word will be a problematical measure here, in a passage that speaks precisely of a break
with meaning. In fact, tracing the word "cruelty" to its etymological
origins, through the Latin *crudelitas* from *crudelis*, and through *crudus*
meaning raw, one arrives at its concrete significance—*cruor*, meaning
blood, and *kreas* (from the Greek), meaning flesh. A rather untenable
conclusion amidst the repeated assertions that cruelty cannot be made
synonymous with blood and flesh.

This contradiction places us farther than ever from a *definition* of
"cruelty," yet it indicates at least the way in which the word can be
expected to operate. What takes place (Artaud would say "in space")[6]
in this passage is a scene in the theater of cruelty, a scene in which

---

It is not a question in this Cruelty either of sadism or of blood, at least not exclusively.
(*Théâtre*, p. 120)

One can very well imagine a pure cruelty, without carnel laceration. (*Théâtre*, p. 121)

Cruelty is not in fact a synonym of spilled blood, of martyred flesh. (*Théâtre*, p. 121)

This word cruelty must be taken in a broad sense and not in the material sense. . . . And
doing this I claim the right to break with the usual sense of language, to sunder the
frame once and for all, to burst the yoke, to return finally to the etymological origins of
language that, through abstract concepts, always evoke a concrete notion.

cruelty is not simply the referent but the functioning of its textuality. If Artaud ruptures the ordinary meaning of language, it is indeed through the etymology he proposes, by pursuing the true meaning of language according to its origin with rigorous logic. Yet he effects this break, not by arriving at an origin of cruelty that would lie outside of the word, but at the cruelty of the origin. For the "blood" and "flesh" in which the etymological reasoning culminates (as did the rejected material meaning) imply both the contradiction in the stated intention of Artaud's letter and the impossibility of distinguishing between the "*sens usuel*" and a break with it. If one insists, however, on marking a distinction between the two, as Artaud apparently does, so that the passage may seem to have some sense of logical progression, it may be said to move from "blood" in a "material sense" to "blood" as a "concrete notion"; that is, the notion (word) has become concrete, resistant to understanding and cruel in its repetition.[7]

Yet why should the initiation into *Héliogable* take place by way of *The Theater and Its Double?* To what extent can the scene of cruelty cited above be said to serve as a model for cruelty as it functions in the novel, in which, certainly, no passage plays itself out in an identical way. Despite the manifesto form in which Artaud deliberately cloaks *The Theater and Its Double,* a reading of the first of the "Letters on Cruelty" showed its contents to be anything but manifest, and whatever analogies may link it to *Héliogabale,* it cannot be said to discursively relate the theory behind it.

If *The Theater and Its Double* works as the double of *Héliogabale,* it is only in so far as this double operates similarly to the "hieroglyph" of "On the Balinese Theater."

> Ces acteurs avec leurs robes géométriques semblent des hiéroglyphes animés. Et il n'est pas jusqu'à la forme de leurs robes qui déplaçant l'axe de la taille humaine, ne crée à côté des vêtements de ces guerriers en état de transe et de guerre perpétuelle, des sortes de vêtements symboliques, des vêtements seconds, qui n'inspirent, ces robes, une idée intellectuelle, et ne se relient par tous les entrecroisements de leurs lignes à tous les entrecroisements des perspectives de l'air. (*Théâtre*, p. 65)

These actors with their geometric robes seem animated hieroglyphs. And it is the very form of their robes that, displacing the axis of the human figure, creates next to the garments of these warriors in a state of trance and of perpetual war, sorts of symbolic garments, second garments, that inspire, these robes, an intellectual idea, and connect with one another by all the intercrossings of their lines to all the intercrossings of the perspectives of air.

The actor's robe renders him a hieroglyph by robbing him of his center, by shifting the axis of the human figure. This displacement by the hieroglyph results from a violent "cutting," a *"taille"* of the human.[8] He therefore remains in a state of trance and perpetual conflict. And not only do the form of the robes displace the human center, they create yet another set of symbolical garments, that in turn enter into apparently limitless intercrossings with their surroundings.[9] This endless layering of symbolical strata creates the semblance of a certain meaning, but one that then violently denies its own apparent logic.[10] "These spiritual signs have a precise sense that only strikes us intuitively, but with enough violence to render useless all translation into a logical and discursive language" (*Théâtre*, pp. 65f.).

In its relationship to *Héliogabale*, the "Letter on Cruelty" operates analogously to the hieroglyph. It displaces the novel rather than revealing its unified concept presents it in a state of perpetual contradiction and, in turn, exercises a violence upon us, such that no translation into a discursive language can take place. It was in just this manner that the scene of cruelty in the "Letters on Cruelty" functioned. While alleging to define "cruelty," it rejects the material meaning of the term that would provide the most immediate understanding of the historical events of *Héliogabale*. It then imposes the hard necessity of a logic that claims to explain the origins of the novel's language, but which, when rigorously followed, comes to no conclusion other than a self-invalidation. This self-destructive logic would be the best approximation to a definition of cruelty, if it didn't rule out the possibility of definition.

Now the reader is as "initiated" as he will ever be into *Héliogabale*, for according to Artaud: "one is never initiated into anything but operations, rites, exterior signs, and hieroglyphic passwords that place us on the path [*la voie*] of the secret" (p. 93). Having been placed on the path [*la voie*] of the secret of cruelty and anarchy, his initiation places him no less on *la voix* [the voice], stifling the source of the definition as he unearths nothing but rites, signs, and hieroglyphs. Initiation then, if it indeed provides some introduction into the principles of the text, precludes the possibility of designating a genuine point of origin.

Why set out on the path of *The Theater and Its Double* if only to stifle the voice of theoretical reason? Why not problematize the question of origin in *Héliogabale* discursively rather than theoretically? Perhaps because Artaud writes ironically of the reader/onlooker who requires this discursive literality. In "On the Balinese Theater," for those who are exhausted by the continual, violent, doubling play of the hieroglyphic garments, there appears a realistic double of the human actor.

> Et pour des amateurs de réalisme à tout prix, qui se fatigueraient de ses allusions perpétuelles à des attitudes secrètes et détournées de la penseé, il reste le jeu eminémment réaliste du double qui s'effare des apparitions de l'au-delà. Ces tremblements, ces glapissements puérils, ce talon qui heurte le sol en cadence suivant l'automatisme même de l'inconscient déchaîné, ce double qui, à un moment donné, se cache derrière sa propre réalité, voilà une description de la peur. (*Théâtre*, p. 66)

The embodied double acts out his fears of an apparition from the beyond, yet at a given moment hides himself "behind his own reality," the original figure whom he doubles. And so he himself becomes the "apparition" that threatens to appear—*not* from the outside, but as the rending of the original figure from within.

This scene then indicates not only Artaud's ironical use of literal representations of the fearful, but within the scheme of such literality, a displacement into that hieroglyphic violence it pretended to escape. Certainly, the gesture toward etymology in the "Letter on Cruelty" led to similar conclusions. We should now be ready to enter into the body proper of *Héliogabale*.

THE ORIGINS OF HÉLIOGABALE

> ... *dans ce mélange varié de semences, il y a une volonté et de l'ordre. Il y a même de l'unité, une sorte de mystérieuse logique qui ne va pas sans cruauté.* (*p. 81*)

One might say of *Héliogabale*, for several reasons, what Artaud notes about the religion of the sun. "This religion of the sun, like all

---

And for the amateurs of realism at any price who would become weary of these perpetual allusions to postures that are secret and turned away from thought, there remains the eminently realistic game of the double who is startled by the apparitions from the beyond. These tremblings, these puerile yappings, this heel that knocks against the ground in a cadence following the very automatism of the unleashed unconscious, this double who at a given moment hides himself behind his own reality, there is a description of fear.

... in this varied mixture of semen there is a will and order. There is even unity, a sort of mysterious logic that cannot function without cruelty.

that concerns ancient Paganism—one doesn't know by which end to grab it" (p. 475). Although it begins with the circulation of sperm surrounding his birth and ends with the circulation of blood and excrement surrounding his death, it would not be rigorously correct to characterize the text as either linear or circular.

Any interpretation must orient itself to an apparently chaotic succession of anecdotal details in order to find the necessity of this chaos and of the turning from occidental thought[11] required by this orientation. Only in this way can it attempt a "logical image" (p. 475). What follows then is a somewhat forced channeling of the themes of the novel, the reasonable if naive struggle to keep them pure from one another that will, it is true, not so much reduce the disorder of the text as play upon its systematic nature. By no means should this be interpreted as an endeavor to assimilate all of *Héliogabale*: if anything it will rather be a commentary on the very impossibility.

The anarchic structure of the book closely corresponds to the first "theme," the origins of Héliogabale, which (although the issue cannot be pursued here) may also be considered the theme of themes: for Artaud relentlessly insists on the impossibility of tracing back Héliogabale's lineage in such a way that any *arché* may be firmly established.

As the initiation will have made evident, the sperm alluded to in the opening sentence of the novel are the signs and hieroglyphs that surround and obscure the source of Héliogabale: ". . . there is surrounding his cradle an intense circulation of sperm" (p. 15). Although I will attempt to number and account for them, it is not by means of multiplicity alone that the names of Héliogabale's possible ancestors, those excessive signs disseminated throughout the text, render themselves ultimately indecipherable. Nor will it be a question of reducing the elusion of the origin to a particular structure, such as inversion or displacement. Rather I will have to trace out this illusion within concrete passages, where the means of dissembling the true lineage are at least as varied as the texts themselves.

The identity of Héliogabale's mother would seem unmistakable, for at almost every point of reference to her in the novel, and in the historical sources, she is called Julia Soaemias. The single exception, remarkably enough, is Artaud's initial reference to her.

> Car, si Bassianus fait deux filles, Julia Domna et Julia Moesa; Julia Moesa
> à son tour fait deux filles: Julia Soemia et Julia Mammoea. Et Julia
> Moesa, avec pour mari Sextus Varius Marcellus, mais sans doute fécon-

dée par Caracalla ou Geta (fils de Julia Domna, sa soeur) ou par Gessius Marcianus, son beau-frère, l'époux de Julia Mammoea; ou peut-être par Septime Sévère, son arrière-beau-frère; enfante . . . Héliogabale. (p. 16)

Paule Thévenin, playing the role of the scientific editor, notes with some surprise the total misreprensentation of this genealogy.

Antonin Artaud s'est quelque peu embrouillé dans la généalogie d'Héliogabale. Julia Moesa est sa grandmère, et si elle est bien la soeur de Julia Domna, elle n'est ni la femme de Sextus. . . . Du reste partout ailleurs, Antonin Artaud indiquera qu'Héliogabale était fils de Julia Soemia et petit-fils de Julia Domna. (p. 388)

Yet his initial entanglement of the genealogical tree can hardly be insignificant, and the maternal source of Héliogabale is, no less than the paternal, multiple. "If History . . . gives him as the son of his mothers, it is because surrounding his cradle there were four mothers" (p. 313). "There is surrounding this son of a coach driver . . . a Pleiad of Julies" (p. 15). It is no coincidence that the formulation "There is surrounding" repeats that of the opening lines—("there is surrounding his cradle an intense circulation of sperm")—for Julia Soaemias, as her name suggests, functions not only as the womb but also as the semen, and as the sign (*Séméion*)[12] of the origin of Héliogabale that generates and differentiates itself into four variations of Julies. This differentiation of Soaemias's name confuses quite a bit what seemed to be the unambiguous trace of lineage through the mother, the single value of which was to *fix* the name: ". . . the maternal filiation had value only with respect to the name" (p. 314).

Assigning an identity to (which amounts to giving identity to the sign of) Héliogabale through his male ancestor is an equally critical problem.

For if Bassianus produces two daughters, Julia Domna and Julia Maesa, Julia Maesa in turn produces two daughters, Julia Soaemias and Julia Mamaea. And Julia Maesa, with Sextus Varius Marcellus as her husband, but no doubt impregnated by Caracalla or Geta (son of Julia Domna, her sister) or by Gessius Marcianus, her brother-in-law, husband of Julia Mamaea, or perhaps by Septimius Severus, her great-brother-in-law, gives birth to . . . Héliogabale.

Antonin Artaud is quite a bit confused in the genealogy of Héliogabale. Julia Maesa is his grandmother, and if she is indeed the sister of Julia Domna, she is neither the wife of Sextus. . . . Moreover, everywhere else Antonin Artaud indicates that Héliogabale was the son of Julia Soaemias and grandson of Julia Domna.

> ... il y a autour de son berceau une intense circulation de sperme.
> Héliogabale est né à une époque où tout le monde couchait avec tout le
> monde; et on ne saura jamais où ni par qui sa mère a été réellement
> fécondée. (p. 15)

Although unable to precisely specify the source of sperm, the entan-
gled genealogy soon offers a matrix of candidates. With the exception
of a single member, this list includes all the living males of Bassianus's
lineage.

I will cut off the pursuit of Héliogabale's father rather abruptly
here—at least long enough to pose the question: is the relationship
among these figures in the genealogy really (only) familiar—or is
there, in this spermatic circulation, that which turns the most familiar
and knowable into the excessive and inaccessible?

> Le sperme coule à flots peut-être, mais c'est un fleuve intelligent, que ce
> fleuve de sperme, qui coule et qui sait qui'il ne se perd pas. (p. 41)

Certainly, it is not immediately apparent why the "intelligence" of the
river of sperm should rule out comprehension, or how this flood
relates to Artaud's assertion that the source of the insemination of
Héliogabale's mother will remain unknown. Most difficult to grasp in
this passage is that the sperm, while flowing knows that it does not lose
itself, "sait qu'il ne se perd pas." This is to say, not only that the river
does not lose its way, that it traces an assigned course, but that it is also
conscious (in Artaud's sense of the term) of this rigorous necessity.
Precisely because it must obey this necessity, the sperm refuses to lose
itself in yet another sense of the term, namely, to the reader-historian
who attempts to designate the father and thereby reduce the flow of
the "varied mixture of semen" (p. 81) to a single static source. The
stream, as a perpetual displacement, does not disappear ("il ne se perd
pas"), but continues to gush forth in torrents whose excess defies such
naming.

This interpretation leaves rather vague just how the "intelligence"
of the river differentiates itself from that historical sense of truth that
tries to fix the origin of Héliogabale, but the "Letters on Cruelty"

... there is surrounding his cradle an intense circulation of sperm. Héliogabale was
born in an epoch when everyone slept with everyone, and it will never be known where
or by whom his mother was really impregnated.

The sperm flows in waves perhaps, but it is an intelligent river, this river of sperm, that
flows and knows that it doesn't lose itself.

provide a useful term, analogous to intelligence. "The cruelty is above all lucid, it's a sort of rigid direction, submission to necessity. There is no cruelty without consciousness, without a sort of applied consciousness" (*Théâtre*, p. 121). The lucidity of the river operates as submission to the necessity of a rigid direction, a lucidity that Artaud calls here "applied consciousness." If the applied consciousness is, as the etymology of "applied " suggests, a twined or twisted consciousness, this application hardly implies the perfect coincidence of consciousness with that onto which it folds. The latter would function precisely as the structure of that historical consciousness that comes from the outside to seek the truth of its object. But Artaud's "applied consciousness," if it may indeed be said to be conscious of something, knows that it must submit to the cruelty of "direction." It is the consciousness of authority ceaselessly shifted away from itself as it yields to movement in a particular direction. It might be called the consciousness of the loss of consciousness, although the phrase tends toward meaninglessness or, more rigorously, a consciousness that, applying cruelty to itself, perpetually cancels itself.

This operation may be attributed to the "intelligence" of the river of sperm, which is, as we have seen, a river of signs—those names sowed throughout the text as the possible if improbable fathers of Héliogabale. The "intelligence" (from inter—between, and *legere*, *legein*—to read, say) of the flow of signs is the displacement from one to another, a saying or reading between the names, the play of the current of the text itself that is constantly in motion and unable to fix upon any of its signs as giving access to an origin.

The circulation of sperm, then, that surrounds Héliogabale's cradle is no orderly circular movement periodically returning back to its origin, but rather a perpetual spending. Nowhere is this better enlarged upon than in the lengthy scene describing the circulation of that other river alluded to in the initial line of the novel (if not directly named), the Tiber as it sweeps Héliogabale's cadaver out to sea. This is the final, if explicitly inconclusive, passage of *Héliogabale*.

S'étant bien repue de sang et de la vue obscène de ces deux corps dénudés, ravagés, et qui montrent tous leurs organes, jusqu'aux plus secrets, la troupe essaie de faire passer le corps d'Héliogabale dans la première bouche d'égout rencontrée. Mais si mince qu'il soit, il est encore trop large. Il faut aviser.

On a déjà ajouté à Elagabalus Bassianus Avitus, autrement dit Héliogabale, le sobriquet de Varius, parce que formé de semences multiples et issu d'une prostituée; on lui a donné par la suite les noms de

Tibérien et de Traîné, parce que traîné et jeté dans le Tibre après qu'on a essayé de le faire entrer dans l'égout; mais arrivé devant l'égout, et parce qu'il a les épaules trop larges, on a essayé de le limer. Ainsi, on a fait partir la peau en mettant à vif le squelette que l'on tient à laisser intact; et l'on aurait pu alors lui ajouter les deux noms de Limé et de Raboté. Mais une fois limé, il est encore trop large sans doute, et on balance son corps dans le Tibre qui l'entraîne jusqu'à la mer, suivi à quelques remous de distance, du cadavre de Julia Soemia.

Ainsi finit Héliogabale, sans inscription et sans tombeau.... [U]ne telle vie, qu'une mort pareille couronne, se passe, il me semble de conclusion. (pp. 136-37)

Implicit in the river of sperm was the figure of the historian attempting to fix the name of the father, to put an end to the scandal of so many sperm and the uninterpretable gliding of signs. This moral figure is not unrelated to the police of the final passage, who, having killed their emperor, have now had more than their fill of the obscenity of his cadaver, the excessive vestiges of Héliogabale. Quite literally satiated (*repue*), they attempt to force another mouth ("the first sewer mouth they encounter") to digest and reduce the body to traceless excrement.

"But . . . he is still too broad": in what sense broad? The second of the three paragraphs cited above, notes a type of ungovernable addition that exceeds the measure of Héliogabale's shoulders, the apparently endless addition of signs. Not only has the multiple sperm that formed Héliogabale led to a proliferation of his name (Varius) but the very attempt to eliminate his remains has added the names of Tibérian and Traîné and the possibility of two others. It is no coincidence

---

Being quite satiated with blood and with the obscene sight of these two denuded and ravaged bodies that show all their organs, even the most secret ones, the troop tries to push the body of Héliogabale into the first sewer mouth they encounter. But, as slender as it is, it is still too broad. They had to deal with it.

They had already added to Elagabalus Bassianus Avitus, otherwise called Héliogabale, the nickname of Varius, because formed from multiple sperm and issue of a prostitute: they had given him later the names of Tiberian [*Tibérien*] and Dragged [*Traîné*] because he was dragged and thrown into the Tiber after they had tried to push him into a sewer: but having reached the sewer, and because his shoulders are too broad, they tried to file him down [*le limer*]. Thus they separated the skin, exposing the skeleton, which they insist on leaving intact; and they could have added to it the two names of Filed [*Limé*] and Polished [*Raboté*]. But once filed he is without doubt still too broad, and they heave his body into the Tiber that drags him along to the sea, followed several swirls away by the cadaver of Julia Soaemias.

Thus Héliogabale comes to an end, without inscription and without a tombstone.... [S]uch a life, crowned by such a death, dispenses with a conclusion, it seems to me.

that these last two terms, traces of a final effort to file and plane down
Héliogabale, are both used in expressions meaning "to polish one's
style" (*limer son style, raboter son style*); for the maneuvers of the police to
eradicate the chaotic and extravagant signs of Héliogabale would be
akin to an effort to reduce that perpetual play of signs taking place in
the river of sperm to a style ruled by convention and narrow logic.
But, as Artaud repeatedly insists, "it [his style] is ... too broad."

Perhaps this interpretation becomes less exorbitant than it seems in
light of a passage from the appendix in which Artaud weaves together
the unpolished style of his own narration and the problematical nature of Héliogabale's lineage.

> Je (ne) me suis engagé à rien de précis, et surtout pas à conduire mon
> récit d'une façon plutôt que de l'autre, et que si j'ai une rédaction cir-
> culaire et en spirale où la pensée sans cesse a l'air d'en revenir sur la
> pensée, il faut s'en prendre tout d'abord à la forme de mon esprit qui me
> donne déjà assez de fil à retordre comme cela. . . . Il faut prendre ce livre
> tel qu'il est ou le rejeter sans ambages, et si l'on accepte accepter même
> l'amphigouri et la redondance des pages qui suivent et qui décrivent sur
> le mode littéraire l'état physique et philosophique de la Syrie après la
> décomposition du royaume des Séleucides, et l'éviction des Sam-
> sigéramides du trône solaire d'Emath. (p. 323)

The composition of the text works in circular and spiral fashion,
which is to say that although seeming to return to a point of origin, it
continually becomes displaced in a spiral. Its thought seems to return
to itself and yet to "revenir sur la pensée" in the sense of going back on
its thought, much as one goes back on one's word. This results in
nonsense and redundancy, a repetitious superfluity of words that in
no way contributes to the meaning of the text, an excess of signs we
noted elsewhere in *Héliogabale*. Artaud lays the blame on the form of
his mind "qui me donne déjà assez de fil à retordre." In light of the
"applied consciousness," this recurring image of twined yarn, al-

---

I have not bound myself to anything precise, and certainly not to conducting my
narrative in one manner rather than in another, and if I have a circular and spiral
composition in which thought seems incessantly to go back on thought, the blame must
be laid first of all on the form of my mind, that already gives me enough trouble as it is
[*qui me donne déjà assez de fil à retordre comme cela*]. . . . You must take this book as it is or
reject it without circumlocution, and if you accept it, you must accept even the amphigouri and the redundance of the pages that follow and that describe in the literary
manner the physical and philosophical state of Syria after the decomposition of the
realm of the Seleucidae and the eviction of the Samsigeramides from the solar throne
of Emath.

though camouflaged as ordinary idiom, cannot be without significance. For Artaud's mind—his thought or text—operating as that
lucid cruelty referred to in the "Letters on Cruelty," moves by a twist-
ing upon itself that results in amphigouri. The determination of
meaning is not directed by the external intention of the writing consciousness: ". . . I have not bound myself . . . to conducting my narrative in one manner rather than in another" (p. 323).

Such dispossession of authority in the composition of the novel is
paralleled by the decomposition of the Seleucidian realm. The passage describes a Syria from whose throne the ancestors of
Héliogabale, the Samsigeramides, have been evicted, marking a break
with Héliogabale's origins, and here, as elsewhere, Héliogabale signifies the novel no less than the historical figure.

As will soon be evident, there is no better point of reference than
this dispossession of the text's author to return the commentary to the
question of Héliogabale's father, and more specifically to that entan-
gled genealogy, only half of which was cited earlier (p. 50).

> Et Julia Moesa, avec pour mari Sextus Varius Marcellus, mais sans doute
> fécondée par Caracalla ou Geta (fils de Julia Domna, sa soeur) ou par
> Gessius Marcianus, son beau-frère; l'époux de Julia Mammoea; ou peut-
> être par Septime Sévère, son arrière-beau-frère; enfante Varius Avitus
> Bassianus, plus tard surnommé Elagabalus, ou fils des sommets, faux
> Antonin, Sardanapale, et enfin Héliogabale. (p. 16)

The long list of names now seems quite literally a stream of sperm/
signs: and perhaps there is nothing to be concluded from the multiplicity of fathers that was not already accounted for by the play of the
"intelligent" river.

If the citation has been extended to include several of the many
names of Héliogabale, it is to test the logical assumption of a traceable
correspondence between the names of father and son. The most striking of the possibly inherited names is "Antonin," precisely because of
the adjective *"faux,"* which already severs any smooth lineage. The
name might be attributed to the husband of Soaemias, who, later in
the text, is called Varius Antoninus Macrin (p. 41), or to Caracalla,

---

And Julia Maesa, with Sextus Varius Marcellus as her husband, but no doubt impregnated by Caracalla or Geta (son of Julia Domna, her sister) or by Gessius Marcianus,
her brother-in-law, husband of Julia Mamaea, or perhaps by Septimius Severus, her
great-brother-in-law, gives birth to Varius Avitus Bassianus, later named Elagabalus, or
son of the summits, false Antonin, Sardanapalus, and finally Héliogabale.

who, at one point, is named Antonin Caracallus (p. 81), or to the fact that Héliogabale is said to succeed to the Antonins.[13] The multiplicity of possibilities already gives "Antonin" the same status as "Varius," marking a disparity rather than certainty of origin.

Yet this excludes the exceedingly obvious explanation of "Antonin," of which Artaud's correspondance does not fail to speak—Antonin Artaud.[14] Thoroughly irritated by Jean Paulhan's queries into the historical veracity of the facts of Héliogabale's life, he writes the following two confessions as to the true identity of his hero.

> Vrai ou non le personnage d'Héliogabale vit, je crois, jusque dans ses profondeurs, que ce soient celles d'Héliogabale personnage historique ou celles d'un personnage qui est moi. Vous qui avez aimé de moi des choses moins vivantes ... je ne comprends pas que ce livre où je pense m'être réalisé avec mes défauts, mes outrances et aussi les qualités que je puis avoir provoque vos résistances. (Letter of June 1, 1934, p. 185)

> Vous avez peut-être raison; il se peut que ce livre soit moins vrai que d'autres oeuvres qui j'ai faites; en ce sens qu'il est moins direct et que j'ai dû prendre un détour pour m'exprimer. Mais tout compte fait je crois que je m'y suis tout de même et mon moi direct et pesant. Il y a une gangue, c'est sûr; mais je finis tout de même par m'y rejoindre dans le détail de maints et maints passages, et dans la conception de la figure centrale où je me suis moi-même décrit. (Letter of August 20, 1934, pp. 187f.)

The context of the first letter leaves no doubt that Artaud is once again out to dupe the reader who has read him with such a literal eye. The opening paragraphs of that letter emphasize the naiveté of such limited notions of objective representation, and each time the cited passages specifically assert the identity of Héliogabale and Antonin Artaud, they preface the remark by placing the "truth" of the text in

---

True or not, the character of Héliogabale lives, I believe, into his depths, whether they be those of Héliogabale the historical character or those of a character who is myself. You have loved things in me that were less alive ... I do not understand how this book in which I think to have realized myself with my faults, my excesses, and also those qualities I may have, provokes your resistance. (p. 185)

You are perhaps right, it is possible that this book is less true than other works I have created, in the sense that it is less direct and that I had to make a detour in order to express myself. But all things considered I believe that I observe myself there nevertheless—my self, direct and weighty. There is a gangue, for sure, but I end up nevertheless by joining myself in the detail of many passages and in the conception of the central figure in which I have described myself. (pp. 187f.)

doubt ("True or not, the character of Héliogabale," ". . . this book is less true than other works"). If Artaud may be said at all to be "realized" (p. 185) in *Héliogabale,* it is as a continual deviation that empties out his self ("a detour in order to express myself" [p. 187]), as the play of absence (*défaut* [p. 185]), and excess (*outrance* [p. 185]), that we have seen to take place.

> . . . je me demande toujours de quel vrai on me parle, et jusqu'à quel point la notion qu'on peut avoir d'un vrai limité et objectif ne cache pas l'autre qui obstinément échappe à tout cerne, à toute limite, à toute localisation. (p. 184)

If not in Artaud, the long probe into Héliogabale's ancestry can be brought to an end in Bassianus. He is the figure repeatedly put forward as the initial member of the dynasty—though not without some reservations with respect to the historical knowledge gained.

> Tenterons-nous de percer le mystère des origines de ce Bassien avec lequel commence l'éphémère dynastie des Bassianides. . . . Historiquement . . . l'opération semble impossible, et ce travail de fiches n'a pas d'attrait pour nous. Il ne nous apprendrait rien. (p. 303)

It teaches us nothing because Bassianus, father of the line, is also a "parricide," signifying then no less the annihilation than the establishment of the father.

> Mais pour en revenir aux Bassiens, dont Héliogabale est le plus illustre, et dont Bassianus est le fondateur, il y a un terrible hiatus entre la lignée des Bassiens, et celle des Samsigéramides; et cet hiatus est marqué par une usurpation et par un crime, qui détournent sans l'interrompre la descendance du soleil. (p. 20)

I ask myself continually of what truth they speak to me and to what degree the notion they might have of a limited and objective truth hides the other notion that obstinately escapes all encirclement, all limit, all localization.

Let us try to pierce the mystery of the origins of this Bassian who begins the ephemeral dynasty of the Bassianides. . . . Historically . . . the operation seems impossible and this index-card labor has no attraction for us. It would not teach us anything.

But to return to the Bassians of whom Héliogabale is the most illustrious, and of whom Bassianus is the founder, there is a terrible hiatus between the lineage of the Bassians and that of the Samsigeramides; and this hiatus is marked by a usurpation and by a crime, that turns aside the descendance of the sun without interrupting it. (p. 20)

... entre Bassianus ... et le dernier roi solaire d'Emèse se recontre un fossé. ... Car il y a, ne l'oublions pas, à l'origine de la dynastie des Bassiens fondée par ce Bassanius d'Emèse, un parricide sur lequel l'Histoire glisse sans insister. (p. 336)

En ce qui concerne Bassianus, un fait est certain, c'est que, dans la lignée héréditaire des prêtres-rois d'Emath, il y a une coupure très nette. (p. 309)

Just how to describe the "hiatus" and "cutting" is a rather delicate problem. We can get around it temporarily by noting at least the more abstract implications of Bassianus's profession, before he assumed the role of patriarch. "The father of them all [Bassianus], the feminine source of this river of rapes and infamies, was supposed to have been a coach driver [*cocher de fiacre*] before being a priest (p. 15). Not only was Bassianus a *cocher,* but he in turn traces his ancestry from a coach driver.

N'est-il pas plausible de croire que ce Bassianus n'était pas le fils illégitime de Samsigéramus mais de sa femme, et que celle-ci ayant fauté avec un cocher a voulu éloigner du Sacerdoce l'enfant adultérin. (p. 313)

Yet this originary source of the family is no less *cocher* than *coché,* which is to say that he is marked with a *coche*—a stroke that cuts into and removes a part of the name it tallies. Bassianus is thus threatened with being crossed out by the same sign that checks him off and affirms him as the source of a line, a sign recorded by the new generation. Similarly, Bassianus was son both of a *cocher* and of a *coché,* for, as his double role of father and parricide will already have indicated, his father suffered a violent cutting: " ... (Bassianus), in order to reach the throne did not fear butchering his direct ancestors" (pp. 307f.). This then sets the pattern for the generation of Héliogabale, a reproduc-

---

... between Bassianus ... and the last solar king of Emesa there is a ditch. ... Because there is, let us not forget it, at the origin of the dynasty of the Bassians, founded by this Bassianus of Emesa, a parricide over which History glides without insisting on it. (p. 336)

Concerning Bassianus, one fact is certain, it's that in the heriditary lineage of the priest-kings of Emath, there is a very clear cutting. (p. 309)

Isn't it plausible to believe that this Bassianus was not the illegitimate son of Samsigeramus but of his wife, and that she, having fallen into sin with a coach driver wished to remove the adulterine child from the priesthood.

tion taking place from origins already vulgar that produces descendants only by rupturing their source.

The significance of this cutting and vulgarity linked to generation has hardly been exhausted. A passage from the appendix brings together the turn of generations, the *cochers/cochés*, and an indirect recommendation from Artaud as to their interpretation.

> Le vieux royaume d'Emath est, nous l'avons dit, réduit à un temple. Si à l'intérieur de ce temple Bassianus, fils de cocher, et ancien cocher lui-même, est roi, il n'a guère à l'extérieur, et en face de Septime Sévère, que quelques droits très légers de remonstrance, dont il n'aurait d'ailleurs garde de se servir.
>
> C'est là que se fondra le sens des Métaphores les plus grossières et explosives, directement saisies, directement assimilées. (p. 322)

As in the relationship between Bassianus and his father (*coché*), Septimius Severus appears on the scene as usurper of his future father-in-law. Although there is apparently nothing very shocking here, Artaud insists on the excessive vulgarity of the passage's metaphors, the sense of which will dissolve if taken too literally, "directement saisies." I have already deviated from the normal interpretation by suggesting the play between *cocher/coché*, and can now push the point a bit further with another, in the context of Héliogabale all too evident, meaning of *coché*—to have been treaded[15] by a male fowl (coincidentally a *cochet*).

> Leur père à tous [Bassianus], la source féminine de ce fleuve de stupres et d'infamies, devait avant d'être prêtre, avoir été cocher de fiacre, car on ne comprendrait pas, sans cela, l'acharnement que mit Héliogabale une fois sur le trône à se faire enculer par des cochers. (p. 15)

The old realm of Emath was, as we have said, reduced to a temple. If at the interior of this temple Bassianus, son of a coach driver and former coach driver himself, is king, outside it and over against Septimius Severus, he has only a few very minor rights of remonstrance that he would be very far from using.

It is there that the sense of the grossest and most explosive Metaphors will dissolve, directly seized, directly assimilated.

The father of them all [Bassianus], the feminine source of this river of rapes and infamies, was supposed to have been a coach driver [*cocher de fiacre*] before being a priest, for without that the desperate eagerness that made Héliogabale, once on the throne, have himself sodomized [*se faire enculer*] by coach drivers wouldn't be understandable.

Bassianus is then the *bas anus* (base anus) from which Héliogabale descends and whom he imitates. And the repeated references to *fiacres*[16] are no less innocent.

> Saint Fiacre: Son culte est très populaire. Si en Alsace, il passe pour guérir la syphilis, il est surtout réputé pour la guérison des hémorroides, autrefois appelées le "mal de S. Fiacre," peut-être en vertu d'un jeu de mots: le rapprochement de son nom avec *fic, fistule*.[17]

Yet a too literal interpretation of the function of such plays, here, as above, will simply dissolve the passage's explosiveness. When Artaud writes of "the grossest and most explosive metaphors," it is certainly not the pornographic *content* of anal intercourse or homosexuality to which he refers, for this content would be a limited inversion of a moral code, the simple replacing of one *arché* by another. The passage rather sets into motion an endless chain of inversions, ironizing precisely that logic of literality in favor of a perpetual perversion of meaning. The traceability of Héliogabale's homosexual taste for coach drivers to his father's first profession would imply a smooth linkage and repeatability between generations, analagous to the structure of causality that governs the naive logic of a literal reading—the assumption of a nonproblematic link between a sign and its signification.

Héliogabale's perversions are far less attributable to Bassianus's coach driving than to the dissemination of *cocher/coché/coché/cochet* and Bassianus/*bas anus*.[18] And if these terms establish a connection between the patriarch and son, they are also the means of its dislocation. Each word play indicates, through the act of reproduction, the debasing or attack on that which, as origin, may be called the *arché*. Yet, as the return to an already cited passage will show, the violence practiced on the father is no simple destruction: ". . . this hiatus is marked by a usurpation and by a crime that turn aside [*détournent*] the descendance of the sun without interrupting it" (p. 20). The nature of this hiatus should now be unmistakable. It has been taken over by a criminal misuse, as the etymology of usurpation suggests: the *coche* thus inflicted by the son castrates the father and renders him "the feminine source" (p. 15). The hiatus between generations does not, therefore,

---

Saint Fiacre: His cult is very popular. If in Alsace he is credited with curing syphilis, he is especially well known for the curing of hemorrhoids, once called the "malady of Saint Fiacre," perhaps by virtue of a play on words, the closeness of his name with *fic, fistule*.

mark a complete break, but merely turns aside [*détourne*] the descendance. In what sense *détourne*? The meaning of descendance is first of all twisted to mean degenerate, low. The father is *inverti,* turned into a deviate. The origin has been displaced.

As here, throughout *Héliogabale,* the questions of origin and lineage that never cease to circulate are inextricably bound to the question of representation. In this respect, the operation of the term *"cocher"* might even be held as exemplary—if the nature of its operation didn't exclude the possibility of the model. In establishing the link between Bassianus and his image, Héliogabale, its differential significations mark the nonrepeatability of an integral origin.

The conclusions to be drawn for the relation between the critical and literary texts are somewhat scandalous. *Héliogabale* refuses to be set up as a source of meaning to be "directly seized, directly assimilated" (p. 322) by a critical discourse desiring to reveal its sense. Admittedly, this puts the critic in a rather difficult position. Artaud demands an approach to his novel that functions with no less violence than the generation of Bassianus's line, namely, a re-production which usurps the text, attacking it as an *arché* of fixed meaning, and yet which "turns [it] aside . . . without interrupting it." Nothing less is required than an inversion of the text that turns it on its end. The violence we have been tracing in Artaud then is hardly one-sided, for if the critical attack releases into play "the grossest and most explosive metaphors" it implicates itself as much as the literary text in the perversion of sense.

HISTORY: THE ONANIST IDIOT

> *À le replacer dans le temps, ce déploiement innombrable de dieux que les peuples, dans leur avance historique, répandent successivement dans les cieux,—et souvent le même emplacement du ciel visible est occupé par des effigies de nature contraire, . . . —à le replacer dans le temps, ce piétinement autour des principes ne touche pas plus à leur*

To place back in time this countless unfolding of gods that the peoples, in their historical advance, spread out successively in the heavens,—and often the same location of the visible heaven is occupied with effigies of opposing nature . . .—to place it back in time, this trampling around the principles touches their initial validity as little as the masturbations of an onanist idiot touches the principle of reproduction.

> *validité initiale que les masturbations d'un idiot*
> *onaniste ne touchent au principe de la reproduction.*
> —Héliogabale, pp. 59–60

For the sake of logic, I unfolded earlier only a single version of the notion of history. The relationship between the historian and the intelligent river of sperm was organized hierarchically, and history, although never specifically named at that point of Artaud's text, was implicitly present as the naive attempt to escape the flux of signs and to fix definitively the origins of Héliogabale. Yet, such separation and reduction of the notion of history is necessarily in error about its signification: "... the same name ... was used ... for two forms" (p. 60), and the detachment of one signification is only half the story.

Still this side of the story must be more fully related before we can trace the inversion into its opposite. Direct allusions to history are often made by way of ridicule, for the historical texts (from which a great number of passages have been assimilated into the novel) are, as the voice of moral judgment, in direct variance with the narrative voice. "I do not judge that which resulted from it as History might judge it; this anarchy, this debauch pleases me" (p. 21).

This moralizing on the part of history is not unrelated to its attempt to slide over the hiatus in Héliogabale's descendance, a hiatus that was seen to be one of those "grossest and most explosive metaphors" (p. 322).

> ... entre Bassianus, son ancêtre, et le dernier roi solaire d'Emèse se recontre un fossé que l'Histoire ne peut combler. Car il y a, ne l'oublions pas, à l'origine de la dynastie des Bassiens fondée par ce Bassanius d'Emèse, un parricide sur lequel l'Histoire glisse sans insister. (p. 336)

> Deux historiens sur les trois, qui, vivant à l'époque d'Héliogabale, nous parlent de l'hérédité de Bassien, mentionnent, sans trop y insister, ses origines plébéiennes, et pourtant ils le donnent comme l'authentique

---

... between Bassianus, his ancestor, and the last solar king of Emesa there is a ditch that History cannot fill in. Because there is, let us not forget it, at the origin of the dynasty of the Bassians, founded by this Bassianus of Emesa, a parricide over which History glides without insisting on it. (p. 336)

Two out of three historians who, living in the epoch of Héliogabale, speak to us of the heredity of Bassian, mention without insisting too much on it, his plebian origins, and nevertheless they present him as the authentic descendant of an uninterrupted lineage of kings. They note but as though making the cut of which we spoke above and they leave us the trouble of reconciling these insoluble contradictions. (p. 309)

descendant d'une lignée ininterrompue de rois. Ils notent, mais comme
en faisant la coupure dont nous parlions plus haut, et nous laissent le
soin de concilier ces insolubles contradictions. (p. 309)

As has been so often anticipated, the historical text inverts an entire
constellation of conclusions. It plays the moral counterpart to anarchy, reduces the multiplicity and differentiation of the origin, replaces the pattern of reproduction through parricide with an uninter-
ruptable lineage, and, most significantly of all, establishes a system of
lineal representation in which all possibility of contradiction is repressed. This manipulation of Héliogabale's ancestry is, of course, a
defense of its own textual endeavor—the faithful reproduction of the
original historical reality.

The narrator's mockery of the documentary style is best traced in
his enigmatic commentary on Lucian's descriptions of the temple at
Hieropolis. Two and a half pages of citation from Lucian concentrate
their attention on the enormous phalluses in the vestibule before the
building. They are circumscribed by the following criticism.

> Lucien . . . raconte une visite qu'il a faite au temple d'Astarté à Hiérapolis.
>   . . . Rien ne semble l'avoir frappé en dehors d'un pittoresque tout
> extérieur:
>   [*Here follows the long citation from Lucian of which I record only the last
> sentences.*]
> . . . .
>   "Le temple regarde le soleil levant. Par sa forme et sa structure il
> ressemble aux temples construits en Ionie."
>   *C'est ici que l'on sent la femme.* Si au lieu de nous donner une description
> extérieure du temple d'Hiérapolis, et jamais sa description n'est plus
> extérieure que quand il fait mine de *violer* ses entrailles, de s'introduire
> dans ses secrets, Lucien avait eu la moindre curiosité pour les principes,
> il aurait recherché sur les *colonnades* du temple l'origine extra-humaine
> des *sexes pétrifiés de femelle* qui en forment l'ornementation. C'est le prin-
> cipe meme de l'architecture *d'Ionie*. (pp. 31–33, italics mine)

Lucian . . . tells of a visit that he made to the temple of Astarte at Hieropolis.
    . . . Nothing seems to have struck him except a totally exterior picturesqueness:
    [Here follows the long citation from Lucian of which I record only the last sentences.]
. . . .
    "The temple faces the rising sun. By its form and structure it resembles the temples
constructed in Ionia."
    It is here that one smells the woman. If, rather than giving us an exterior description of
the temple of Hieropolis, and never is his description more exterior than when he
makes a show of violating its entrails, of entering its secrets, Lucian had had the least
curiosity about the principles, he would have searched on the *colonnades* of the temple
for the extra-human origin of the petrified *female sexual organs* that form their ornamentation. It is the very principle of the architecture of *Ionia*.

It is here that one senses Artaud's irony. With the same gesture that condemns the exteriority of Lucian's description, he himself adds yet another superficial concrete detail as the essential missing element. Lucian, by neglecting the principles, has failed to search for the female genitals on the columns of the temple. The almost too obvious interpretation, in light of the "War of Principles" (Part II of *Héliogabale*), is that the historical text necessarily remains ignorant of the doubleness of the origin and therefore presents only the phallic aspect of the temple.

Yet Artaud's duplicity goes much farther. If the narrator insists on the extra-human and ornamental nature of the vaginas, it is because a resemblance other than that of simple representation (the basis for the historical text) warrants calling them "the very principle of the architecture of Ionia." These nonsensible similarities must be pursued through a later passage of *Héliogabale,* describing the insignia of Julia Soaemias and two others from Fabre d'Olivet's *De l'état social de l'homme,* so often alluded to in the novel.

Son [Soaemias'] insigne est la *violette "Ioneh,"* la fleur de l'amour et du *sexe,* parce qu'elle s'effeuille comme un sexe. Et sur son épaule la *colombe* "Ionah." (p. 80, italics mine)

C'est à cause du nom de *Yoni,* analogue à celui de *Ioneh,* une Colombe, que cet oiseau a été consacré à la Déese de l'Amour. (p. 421)[19]

Le *Yoni* prend aussi la forme d'une fleur de *violette*; et voilà pourquoi cette fleur, consacrée à Junon, était si chère aus *Ioniens.* (p. 421, italics partly mine)

The narrator elaborates the resemblance between the temple at Hieropolis and those of Ionia through an obscure allusion to other parts of his text where the differentiation of almost identical signs takes place. Each of these signs (italicized above) finds an oblique echo in the narrative commentary on Lucian: *Ioniens/Ionie*; *Yoni/sexes . . . de femelles*; *Ioneh, violette/C'est ici qu'on* sent *la femme, violer*; *Ionah, Colombe/colonnades.* Whereas Lucian's documentary description uses the term

---

Her [Soaemias's] insignia is the *violet "Ioneh,"* the flower of love and of the sexual organ, because it sheds its petals like a sexual organ. And on her shoulder the dove [*colombe*] "*Ionah.*" (p. 80).

It is because of the name *Yoni,* analogous to that of *Ioneh,* a dove [*Colombe*] that this bird has been consecrated to the Goddess of Love. (p. 421)

The *Yoni* also takes the form of a *violet* flower; and that is why this flower, consecrated to Juno, was so dear to the *Ionians.* (p. 421)

"Ionia" in its most precise and limited significance, it is immediately
played upon as *Ioneh* and *Yoni* (fragrance and woman) in a sentence
whose reference would otherwise be meaningless: "It is here that one
smells the woman."

It is this assimilation of signs that so radically violates the historical
text's concept of truth—assimilation in the double sense, both as a
relationship of analogy and differentiation between signs and a replacing or devouring of the meaning of one sign by that of the next.
History, as our epigraph has already indicated, prefers to "spread out
successively" in time those effigies of noncoincident meaning that
might otherwise occupy the same site, in order to maintain a fixed,
unambiguous clarity of signification.

> ... je veux dire qu'immédiatement, le même nom ne servait jamais à
> deux formes, si l'on tient à considérer ces formes comme des entités
> véritablement séparées, mais le même nom était souvent la contraction
> de deux formes, faites, semble-t-il, pour se dévorer l'une l'autre. (p. 60)

History, like an onanist idiot, quite literally wastes its seed—involved
in a reproduction that is totally self-affective, that admits no conflicts
with the reality it attempts to duplicate, it lacks the consciousness of
perpetual differentiation from its other, of that excess and cruelty
which I have traced as the mode of reproduction of Bassianus's line.[20]

This definitive distinction between the historical and narrative text
creates a convenient fiction, although it falls into the historical tendency of separation and reduction. It also fails to account for the
narrator's continual manipulation of a historical rhetoric even in
moments, such as those just cited, when he directly attacks that
rhetoric:

> ... ceux qui, comme Héliogabale, sont parvenus à offusquer l'Histoire,
> c'est qu'ils avaient des qualités qui auraient pu changer le cours de l'his-
> toire si les circonstances avaient été pour eux. (p. 50)

The circumstances necessary both to obscure the historical sense of
truth and to change its course are against Héliogabale, but, neverthe-

---

I wish to say that the same name was never used for two forms at once, if one insists on
considering these forms as truly separate entities, but the same name was often the
contraction of two forms, made, so it seems, to devour one another.

... those who, like Héliogabale, have succeeded in obscuring History, it's because they
had qualities that would have been able to change the course of history if circumstances
had been in their favor.

less, are in *Héliogabale's* favor. These circumstances are a certain architectural use of the text, much akin to that used by Nietzsche, such that the scheme of successive, distinct periods of history begins to dislodge at its foundations the notion of representation that it was meant to preserve. For this scheme of successive eras parallels that of the relationship of the historical text to its source—in the case of Artaud's "history," to that of other historical texts—a relationship best described as *démarquage**; this is the other version of the notion of history. Artaud supplements a citation from Photius with the following remark:

> Il faut dire que ce texte de Photius n'est pas lui-même une oeuvre originale, mais qu'il est le démarquage d'un livre perdu, qui, à en juger par le nombre des écrivains qui s'y réfèrent, semble avoir constitué pour les anciens une vraie Bible du Merveilleux; la *Vie d'Isidore* par Damascius. (p. 25)

The original work is a book already lost. Deprived of the mark that would establish its identity, it has been reproduced by another text in a manner leaving its origin untraceable.[21]

TEMPLES: THE ARCHITECTURE OF ANARCHY

The temples of *Héliogabale* serve to illustrate those anomolies that have been seen to specify the functioning of the text, for their sedimentary structure is very akin to the layering of myth on myth and historical text on historical text. These temples, like Artaud's novel, are founded on the ruins of former constructions. It is in these ruins, piled one upon the other according to a strict temporal order, that the *arché*-o-logist, the scientist of the *arché,* expects to find highly structured traces of the past; but building on a foundation of ruins means building "without foundations" and the seeker after truth finds the hierarchical levels leveled.

----

démarquage: the removal of the identification marks from, the removal of a marker (from a book), plagiarism.

It must be said that this text of Photius is not itself an original work but that it is the *démarquage* of a lost book, that, to judge by the number of writers who refer to it, seems to have constituted for the ancients a veritable Bible of the Marvelous—the *Life of Isidore* by Damascius.

... on entasse sans fondations édifices sur édifices, et constructions sur constructions. On pilonne, sans sourciller, férocement, le passé, et si quelque vestige, qui pour nous, pour un archéologue, serait précieux, dépasse par trop ou simplement affleure, on le rase, on nivelle l'ensemble. (p. 466)

The archetectonics of these temples are analogous to the baseless foundations on which they are built. Constructed according to a system of descending spirals, it is a blueprint that deconstructs its own hierarchical plan. "Underneath the ground the temple descends in spirals toward the depths: the rites chambers pile up layered vertically on one another." (p. 36) The spiraling levels enter into a strange harmony with the sacred noises of the temple. Each sound, like the structural stratifications, seems to be superimposed successively on the next, setting up a system of mutual reference. But this harmony of vibrations and echoes excludes the possibility of communication. It puts into play a series of nonintelligible whisperings and noises whose only organizing principle is that of the echo.

> Dans le silence soudainement tombé, on entend des pas, des voix, des allées et venues de toutes sortes dans les chambres souterraines de l'édifice; tout cela formant comme des tranches, des étages superposés de chuchotements et de bruits.
> ... le temple vibre, en harmonie avec les tourbillons stratifiés des soussols.... [L]es veilleurs se passent le mot, donnent de la voix, heurtent des gongs, font gémir des trompes dont les voutes se renvoient les échos. (p. 36)

No element in these rites can escape entering the endless web of analogy. These rituals of harmonizing elements at Emesa all turn about the rapaciousness of the god Elagabalus, for the entire function of the temple is quite literally to feed the god.

... they pile up without foundation edifices on edifices, and constructions on constructions. Without wincing they ferociously pound the past, and if some vestige that would be precious for us, for an archeologist, extends out too far or is simply flush, they raze it, they level it.

In the silence that fell suddenly, steps are heard, voices, the coming and goings in all sorts of subterranean chambers of the edifice, all that forming something like slices, superposed levels of whisperings and noises.
... the temple vibrates in harmony with the stratified whirls of the substratums....
[T]he watchers pass the word to one another, bay, strike the gongs, make the horns moan: the vaults reverberate their echoes.

C'est qu'autour des quatre grands repas rituels du dieu solaire, tourne un peuple de prêtres, d'esclaves, de hérauts, de desservants. Et que ces repas eux-mêmes ne sont pas simples, mais qu'à chaque geste, à chaque rite . . . répond. (pp. 45–46)

It is this same god whom the text, in very similar terms, earlier named "Desire": " . . . and this desire, like Elagabalus himself, is not simple" (p. 22). The desire of Elagabalus operates as an irreducible, paroxysmal noncoincidence of elements. What takes place in the harmonic relationship between different stratifications, in the analogistic relationships of the rituals, in the interweavings of trajectories inside the temple, is a continual violent assimilation (consumption) through assimilation (comparison). Thus, Elagabalus/*Héliogabale* sets into play the assimilating harmony.

LE TIMBRE DÉTIMBRÉ

> *Mais l'important est de créer des étapes, des perspectives de l'un à l'autre langage. Le secret du théâtre dans l'espace c'est la dissonance, le décalage des timbres, et le désenchaînement dialectique de l'expression.*—Théâtre, p. 135

To lay bare the framework of *Héliogabale* and locate the central image the text offers of itself, the "central node of the noise" (p. 326), the "central point" (p. 326) of the intricate web—no passage is more appropriate than that describing the visit of Apollonius of Tyana to Iarchus, "the solar node" (p. 326). To be sure, the anecdote is not an integral part of the novel, but one of those fragments collected in the appendix, and its subject matter has no immediate pertinence to the life of Héliogabale. Yet nothing in *Héliogabale* is so irrelevant that it fails to enter into the harmony of the text: " . . . all that makes a very

---

Around the four large ritual meals of the solar god revolves a people of priests, slaves, heralds, ministers. And these meals themselves are not simple, but to each gesture, to each rite . . . corresponds. . . .

But the important thing is to create stages, perspectives from one language to the other. The secret of the theater in space is dissonance, the staggering of the timbres and the dialectic unchaining of expression.

strange and discordant harmony . . . that one senses [to be] so very far
from the most secret laws of thought" (p. 327).

It is this strange music that the passage presents in the guise of a
complaining soul. The context is not insignificant, since it draws a
parallel between a particular architecture and a voice that destroys its
own intelligibility, between that necessity of structure I have shown to
be one component of cruelty and the tottering of that structure. Apollonius finds an abyss, which, like the temples of Hieropolis and
Emesa, consists of innumerable levels piled one upon the other.

> . . . il a rejoint Iarchas, le noeud solaire,—qui habite un gouffre, grouil-
> lant de niches d'hommes, toutes creusées à même le rocher. Sur une
> muraille d'une fabuleuse hauteur, et à vif, comme une ossature
> d'écorché, des multitudes de cellules de moines, à qui un pan de mur
> manquerait, s'entassent les unes au-dessus des autres, et s'allongent jus-
> qu'à l'infini. (p. 325)

Iarchus brings his visitor to the soul of Palamedes, the Carian counterpart of the Egyptian god Toth.[22] Inventor of the alphabet, of the
musical scale, and of weights and measures, he marks the origin of all
standards of logical communication, systematized art, and scientific
judgment. Yet the lamentation of this source of Logos concerns precisely the obliteration of Logos—of that language and art intended to
represent him. "And it complains . . . about its statue buried not far
from Smyrna . . . , about its name forgotten by Homer—it was named
Palamedes, it seems, among men" (pp. 326–27).

This obliteration of word and reason is traced out in the moaning of
Palamedes, which signals a hunger strangely similar to the endless
desires of Elagabalus.

> . . . quelque chose comme une âme en boule n'arrête pas de gémir et
> d'éructer. Rien de plus étrange d'ailleurs que les borborygmes faits par
> une âme. Cela est plein de musiques sevrées, sevrées de musique
> évidemment, qui ne seraient pas des musiques, mais des sons maigres,

---

. . . he joined Iarchas, the solar node—who inhabits an abyss swarming with niches of
men, all hollowed out of the rock itself. On a wall of a fabulous height, stripped like the
skeleton of a flayed man, multitudes of monks' cells, for which a piece of wall would
seem to be lacking, are piled up on one another and extend infinitely.

. . . something like a globular soul never stops moaning and belching. Moreover, there is
nothing stranger than the rumblings made by a soul. It is full of weaned music, weaned
of music evidently, that would not be music but rather lean sounds, sounds emaciated
by a sort of organic fast, which, the whole day long . . . never cease to struggle for
subtlety. Now this subtlety, completely steeped in love, is absolutely without guile.

des sons émaciés par une sorte de jeûne organique, et qui tout le long du jour . . . ne cessent pas de lutter de subtilité. Or cette subtilité toute trempée d'amour est absolument sans astuce. (p. 326)

This hunger eludes definition because it is itself the movement toward indefinability. Therefore, in the attempts to specify its nature, the music of Palamedes's belching and groaning repeatedly undergoes a certain emaciation, an emaciation that takes place as the breakdown of music's fixable and repeatable structural organization and that finally results in an apparent silence. The intestinal rumblings have already been weaned from any musical origin—cut off so that there is no systematic interrelationship among them determined by rules of conventional harmony: they are sounds rather than music. If they strive with one another for subtlety, this is not to be understood as a rational intentionality, for they are "absolutely without guile," but rather as subtlety in the sense of an erosion of substance. "It is mysticity hollowed out by mysticity" (p. 326), a mysticity that functions like its etymological root *mystos:* keeping silent. The endpoint of the emaciation, then, is not simply mysticity, but the multifold, layered, hollowing out of something akin to silence.

This process involves an "organic fast" that is not only the disintegration of systematic organization but also of the *organe*—the voice—and most especially the voice as faithful representative of human thought.

C'est . . . quelque chose qui ferait penser à une voix aiguë de tête fournie par l'arrière-arrière-gorge, aussi loin qu'une gorge humaine puisse aller dans le recul, et repoussée par la volonté surtendue de la tête encore quelques diapasons plus au fond. Tout nu, ce son, ce timbre, ce diapason, non seulement par leur pureté, mais fourni par une série de feuillets de son, dont chacun est en recul sur l'autre de un, deux ou plusieurs degrés. Tous les quarts de ton du monde sensible mis l'un derrière l'autre et déchirés, ou plutôt soustraits l'un de l'autre, ne sauraient fournir une idée de ce détimbrage atroce et qui finit par donner une sensation de vide et de silence absolue. (p. 326)

It is something that would make you think of a sharp head-voice put forth by the back of the back of the throat, as far as a human throat can go backward, and pushed further back several diapasons deeper by the overstrained will of the head. Completely naked, this sound, this timbre, this diapason, not only as a result of their purity, but put forth by a series of sheets of sound in which each one is set back from the other by one, two or several degrees. All the quarter tones of the tangible world, placed one behind the other and torn or rather subtracted from one another, could not furnish an idea of this atrocious *détimbrage* (dis-timbering, dis-stamping) that ends by giving a sensation of absolute emptiness and silence.

Artaud compares the guttural sounds of Palamedes's soul to a piercing voice that violates the bounds of the human and overstrains the limits of the center of reason—the head. This deconstruction of the origin of Logos by means of a successive movement backward is not unrelated to an all too familiar semblance of structure that permeates the whole. The tone is put forth by a series of sounds whose relationship is not precisely mutual destruction but rather a subtraction of each from the next, a limitless marking of difference that produces an indefinable *détimbrage*, approximated by, but not equivalent to, absolute silence and emptiness.

> ... or dans cette musique gutterale de l'âme, ce timbre détimbré, mais qu'il faut dépeindre ainsi et le fixer dans le caractère que je viens de lui donner, est encore en recul sur d'autres sons et d'autres timbres, il crée avec eux des manières de perspectives, une musique supérieurement organisée, et qui donne des noeuds-stations, ces points d'orgue de la vibration qui font nombre, comme un silence qui est ... le noeud central du bruit, comme le point le plus aigu de la flamme, le point-centre, finit par donner de la nuit, comme Iarchas est le noeud-lumière, le point de recontre de toutes les frictions, de toutes les contradictions. (p. 326)

Because the discordant timbre cannot be fixed, the text is forced to depict it through analogies, of silence, for example, or of quarter tones arranged one behind the other. Yet these "could not furnish an idea of this atrocious *détimbrage*" (p. 326). No image can coincide exactly. The entire description of Palamedes has been articulated from the very beginning by a chain of such assimilations. The very source of the problematic sounds is identified only indirectly as "something *like* a globular soul" (italics mine), whose belchings make one think of a piercing head-voice that, in turn, is not identical to a succession of musical tones. The passage just cited adds to the long list of comparisons.

As impossible as it may be to fix the idea, the "timbre détimbré" is (like) a dis-printed imprint of the text. It is always one step removed

---

... now in this guttural music of the soul, this dis-timbered timbre [*timbre détimbré*], that it is however necessary to thus depict and to fix in the character that I have just given it, [this timbre] is still set back from other sounds and other timbres; it creates with them modes of perspectives, a superiorly organized music, that gives stationary nodes, these vibratory fermatas that produce cadence, something like a silence that is ... the central node of the noise, like the most intense point of the flame, the central point, ends by giving night, since Iarchas is the light node, the point of meeting of all the frictions, of all the contradictions.

from other sounds and imprints and gives to them a semblance of harmonic structure: ". . . it creates with them modes of perspective, a superiorly organized music" (p. 326). No analogy can reify it, because it is itself the movement of analogizing as perpetual differentiation. It is that imprint which makes structure a possibility and the continual tracing of deconstruction as well. It functions as an organizing center only in so far as it is the center of contradiction, vibration, disorganization.[23]

The dis-printed imprint is at work throughout *Héliogabale*, determining its questionable structure while undermining the organizational basis for critical commentary. Although the chaotic fragmentary succession of passages creates an incoherent "noise," they lend themselves—perhaps all too easily—to a chaneling into themes that, by means of their apparent referential content, would seem to open a realm of significance. Yet each of these has articulated separately and systematically the breakdown of order and of those notions of origin, reason, and representation upon which thematic integrity is founded. All themes then, although individually articulated, operate analogously to one another: on this basis of a repeated and similar movement of deconstruction, can I be said to have set up Analogy as a superstructure of the whole? Such a superstructure could in no way escape being just one more link in the discordant chain of analogies. Whatever illusory vantage of perspective may be gained, it necessarily stands in relationship to the other elements, as they do to one another. This is to say that no analogistic formulation is possible, such that it renders present, coincides with, or is reducible to its referent. The attempt to establish a structure holding together the anarchical fragments of the texts necessarily moves toward greater reverberations of anarchy.[24]

THE INCENDIARY ALPHABET

> *Il y a dans toute poésie une contradiction essentielle.*
> *La poésie, c'est de la multiplicité broyée et qui rend*
> *des flammes. Et la poésie qui ramène l'ordre ressuscite*
> *d'abord le désordre, le désordre aux aspects enflam-*
> *més; elle fait s'entrechoquer des aspects qu'elle*
> *ramène à un point unique; feu, geste, sang, cri.*
>
> *Ramener la poésie et l'ordre dans un monde*
> *dont l'existence même est un défi à l'ordre, c'est*

ramener la guerre et la permanence de la guerre;
c'est amener un état de cruauté appliqué, c'est susciter
une anarchie sans nom.—Héliogabale, p. 106

The apocalyptic propensity implicit in the movement of analogy in *Héliogabale* allows the principle strands of our text—those notions of sign, representation, interpretation and origin—to be woven together. From the same description of the Hieropolis temple that was supplemented by the complex play on *Ionie/Ioneh* (violets—the insignia of Soemia)/*Ionah* (dove, carried by Soemia)/*Yoni* (female genitals),[25] Artaud cites the following apparently innocent documentary detail from the historian Lucian:

> "Entre ces deux statues [of Juno and Jupiter], on en voit une troisième également d'or, mais qui n'a rien de semblable aux deux autres. C'est le Séméion; elle porte sur la tête une colombe d'or." (p. 35)

This passage adds to the web of nonreferential similarities that we began to mark out earlier, for Soaemias, whose name almost echoes that of Séméion, like the statue, carries a dove (*Ionah*). Séméion thus functions as a sign for Héliogabale's origin, for Soaemias and, by extension, for the male "multiple sperm" (p. 137). This constellation Séméion/Soaemias/semences is not based on any physical resemblance of the statue to the figures of mother and father, for Séméion, who is both masculine and feminine and neither,[26] "bears no similarity" to the statues of Juno and Jupiter, mother and father of the gods.

In what sense then can Séméion be said to operate as a sign for the origin of Héliogabale? Perhaps not at all—at least not as a sign-*for* the origin. At best, one is left with the formulation, the origin of *Héliogabale* is a sign (σημεῖον), a sign that does not represent but differentiates, that marks the cleft between the masculine and the feminine and creates the space for their continual war. It is a sign

---

In every poesy there is an essential contradiction. Poesy is the pulverized multiplicity that produces flames. And the poesy that brings back order first resuscitates disorder, the disorder with flaming facets; it makes the facets clash with one another which it then brings back to a single point—fire, gesture, blood, cry.

To bring back poesy and order to a world whose very existence is a defiance of order is to bring back war and the permanence of war; it is to bring forth a state of applied cruelty; it is to raise up an anarchy without name.

Between these two statues [of Juno and Jupiter], one sees a third one that is also made of gold but does not resemble the others at all. It is the Séméion. She carries on her head a golden dove.

which, rather than designating a privileged center, itself functions only by being assimilated into a chain of differentiations with other signs. This implies a rather apocalyptic threat to the integrality of the origin and the guarantee of representation traditionally attributed to both sign and origin.

Artaud, as usual, has not faithfully reproduced the historical source he cites, and the original passages from Lucian's *de Dea Syria* give a more precise reference to this catastrophe and Séméion's relationship to it.

> And betwene hem stont a symulacre of gold, not lyk the othere symulacres in no kynde, that hath no propre schap but bereth the qualitees of the other goddes. And the Assuriens hem selve clepen it Tokene, for thei move not seyn whens it cam ne what maner thyng it is. But some beleven, it is of Bachus, and othere that it is of Deucalioun, and othere that it is of Semiramys. And for sothe a dowve of gold stont on his hede, and so their devisen that it is Semiramys Tokene. And it doth iorney twyes eech yeer to the See, for to fecchen that water aforseyde.

The aforesaid water refers to the following earlier passage:

> in here londe opnede a huge hole and resceyvede alle the water; and when this happed, Deucalioun leet maken awteres and let bylden over the hole a temple halowed to Iuno. . . .
>
> In tokene of that storie thei don thus. Twyes eech yeer water cometh fro the See in to the temple. . . . and fro beyonden Eufrate gon manye men to the See and bryngen all watre, that anon thei scheden out in the temple and thanne it goth adoun in to the hole. . . . And in doynge thus thei seyn that Deucalioun made suche ordeynnaunce for the seyntuarye in memorie of that tribulacioun and than benefice.[27]

This peculiar image, the Séméion, whose powers of representation are as indeterminate here as in Artaud's version, is ritually used to reenact the deliverance from Deucalion's flood. Yet the repetition of this scene, the bringing of sea water to dry land at the temple of Hieropolis, is no less interpretable as a reenactment of the flooding than of the deliverance. It is here that the perpetual generation of anarchy lies, not in a reified difference, but in the contradictory operation of the sign both as the apparent redemption through repetition and the instrument of total catastrophe.

The disjoint function of the Séméion is analogous to that of the Baetyls, those magical, usually phallic-shaped stones so frequently punctuating the narrative, for the Baetyls also place into question Héliogabale's origins, a certain solar- and theocentrism and a problematical notion of representation.

La généalogie familiale d'Héliogabale n'a d'intérêt qu'en fonction de ses rapports avec ce globe igné, coeur ardent de notre système terrestre [the sun] à qui les Bétyles ressemblent. . . . Ce n'est pas au hasard, mais pour un nombre on pourrait dire infini d'assimilations spirituelles, qu'Elagabalus, dieu solaire, est représenté par un cône de marbre noir qui s'élève sur un vagin. (p. 316)

It will be no surprise that this chain of assimilations that links together several hierarchical structures—those establishing the priority of the ancestor, of the sun, the gods, and of the penis over the vagina—that this chain is about to be unchained. The weakness of the connection between them, and of each structure in itself, lies in a particular concept of reproduction and imitation.

The gods have created these stones as a direct sign of their own seed, a sign which they have not failed to render inert and unchangeable—the impotent, if concrete, symbol of their own existence and of the firm establishment of their rites.

. . . ils représentent sous un aspect déterminé et fixe la semence même de dieu, ils remontent au temps où les dieux créaient directement des êtres, et sont le signe redevenu inerte de leur formidable expansivité. On les trouve dans tous les lieux où les rites du soleil rayonnent. Ils créent entre la terre et le ciel des manières d'échelons symboliques . . . . On dirait que les dieux ont voulu signifier d'une manière concrète leur désir d'être adorés là. Marquer inoubliablement les lieux où se répandent leurs influences, fixer un terrain pour les rites. (p. 329)

However passive these signifiers of the divine semen are intended to be, it is precisely by virtue of their resemblance to the divine and potent member that a certain usurpation begins to take place. "They are there like an active phallus in the middle of its own sperm" (pp. 316-17). Perhaps something more than usurpation, for the Baetyl,

---

The family geneaology of Héliogabale has no interest except with respect to its relationship with this ignited globe, the burning heart of our terrestrial system [the sun] that the Baetyls resemble. . . . It is not by chance but rather one could say because of an infinite number of spiritual assimilations that Elagabalus, the solar god, is represented by a cone of black marble that rises up on a vagina.

. . . they represent in a determined and fixed perspective the very sperm of god; they go back to the time when the gods created beings directly and are the sign which has once again become inert of their formidable expansivity. They are found in all of the places where the rites of the sun shine forth. They create between the earth and the heavens sorts of symbolic rungs. . . . It would seem that the gods wished to signify in a concrete manner their desire to be adored there. To mark unforgetably the places where their influences gain ground, to fix a terrain for their rites.

rather than itself assuming the theocentric position, threatens to ob-
literate that which established the existence of the god, its sign.

> ... et si leur ardeur s'est momentanément éteinte, ils portent en eux en
> signes incendiares, et gravés par la griffe même de dieu, les paroles
> mortelles, qui au jour de l'Apocalypse entameront la fusion de tous les
> rites, dans le déchaînement d'un alphabet flamboyant. (p. 317)

It is the signature of god, "la griffe même de dieu" that will turn on itself,
no longer representing and reaffirming the presence of the origin,
but rather releasing an apocalyptic, incendiary alphabet, which is no
less an apocalypse *of* the alphabetic, western concept of language.

Yet can this apocalypse actually be relegated to the position of a
future historical era or is the literal interpreter the butt of a certain
jest. If the Baetyls are related to the sun-god Elagabalus and the
genealogy of Héliogabale by an "infinite number of assimilations" (p.
316), they also represent *Héliogabale* in its guise of a textual *arché,* the
text as fixed principle and as origin of meaning, menaced by, and
menacing with, an apocalyptic, but not necessarily deferred, loss of
sense. For the phallic stones, that invariably have a vagina already cut
into—and cutting their base, are the object of an impossible reading.

> Or à la base de cette pierre du ciel qui signifie le membre de l'homme les
> anciens ont cru voir un vagin. Les deux principes rejoints dans une seule
> coulée. L'inextricable union de la dualité primitive qui préside à toute
> création. Or même dans cette union les anciens à la longue n'ont plus su
> lire. (pp. 315–16)

Nowhere is the problematical nature of interpretation made clearer
than by the various anecdotes about the relationship between Eusebius
and his Baetyl, anecdotes taken significantly enough from that same
"lost book" that gave the model for history as *démarquage.* This
historical text, in fact, locates that relationship between the two in our
own era, long before the coming of the apocalypse.

... and if their heat is momentarily extinguished, they carry in them, in incendiary
signs engraved by the very stylus of god, the mortal words that, on the day of the
Apocalypse, will commence the fusion of all the rites in the unchaining of a flaming
alphabet.

Now at the base of this stone from heaven that signifies the human phallus, the ancients
thought they saw a vagina. The two principles in a single casting [*coulée*]. The inextrica-
ble union of the primitive duality that presides over all true creation. Now even in this
union the ancients, in the end, no longer knew how to read.

C'est dans ce mur qu'il déposera la pierre. Elle y restera à demeure jusqu'au jour du dernier jugement, mais d'ici là Eusèbe ne la quittera pas. Et entre Eusèbe et la pierre commence une radieuse histoire humaine, et telle qu'il n'en existait qu'aux grands jours de l'âge d'or. De cette pierre Eusèbe [s'est continué le serviteur, plus que le serviteur,] l'aède, l'interprète mystique, asservi à ses rites. (p. 331)

And that relationship is, of course, that of interpretation, of an interpreter become slave to his textual object, as long as he remains deaf to a certain anarchical laughter answering his own scientific gravity.

Entre Eusèbe et eux [the Baetyls] c'est une bataille constante, une guerre de tous les instants. Ces Bétyles connaissent l'humour et en jouent comme seuls les dieux savent se montrer humoristiques; car en eux l'Esprit parle toutes les langues, et les déceptions qu'ils imposent à leur interprète ont toujours un caractère inspiré. (p. 330)

How seriously,[28] then, should one take this holocaust that menaces the very basis of literary criticism. Only as seriously as I have previously assumed an integral origin of philosophical criticism. Perhaps then humoristically: I am as humoristic as a god can be who is soon to be consumed by a flaming alphabet.

It is in this wall that he will lay the stone. It will remain there permanently until the day of the last judgment, but from this time to that Eusebius will not leave it. And between Eusebius and the stone a radiant human history begins, such as existed only in the great days of the golden age. Eusebius appointed himself the servant of this stone, more than the servant, the bard, the mystical interpreter, a slave to its rites.

Between Eusebius and them [the Baetyls] it's a constant battle, a war of all instants. These Baetyls are versed in humor and play with it in the way that gods alone know to show themselves humorous, and the deceptions that they impose on their interpreter always have an inspired character.

BENJAMIN

Walter Benjamin: Image of Proust

CHAPTER FOUR

> *Das dialektische Bild ist ein aufblitzendes. So, als im Jetzt der Erkennbarkeit aufblitzendes Bild, ist das des Gewesenen . . . festzuhalten. Die Rettung, die dergestalt, und nur dergestalt, vollzogen wird, läßt sich immer nur als auf der Wahrnehmung von dem unrettbar sich verlierenden gewinnen.*
> (Illuminationen, *"Zentral-park," p. 261*)

The journalistic prose of Walter Benjamin's essay "Zum Bilde Prousts" ["Towards the Image of Proust"] presents the uninitiated reader with a deceptive code, for in many places it is Benjamin himself who makes it easy to view his work from the comfortable perspective of conventionally biographical yet undisciplined literary chit-chat. One thread of the argument entangles another, creating an uneven texture of bewildering self-contradiction; as though Benjamin had covered the margins of his galley-proofs with critical self-commentary—but the typesetters, too weary to reset the original text, merely added the new to that which it superseded.

Read as the straightforward discursive text it pretends to be, the essay falls short of the demands currently made on literary criticism. It presents itself as a loose succession of biographical anecdote and casual commentary that attempts to penetrate "to the heart of the Proustian world" (p. 365)[1] by giving the reader apparent access, through the literary work, to the society, the philosophical thought, and the author behind the text. Yet the repeated contradiction and discrepancy that arise from these attempts at penetration offer no sure key to the mastery of Proust's work, and the hermeneutic rigor which the reader of criticism has come to expect remains conspicuously lacking.

The dialectical image is one that flashes. Thus—as an image that flashes in the now of recognizability [*Erkennbarkeit*]—the image of that which has been is . . . to be held fast. The recovery [*Rettung*] that is accomplished in this manner and only in this manner always lets itself be won only as that which irretrievably [*unrettbar*] loses itself in the course of perception [*Wahrnehmung*].

89

It would be reassuring to attribute this looseness to a blindness of the text to its own self-contradiction. Yet if one writes oneself into the logic of Benjamin's metaphorical web, the text itself accounts for the discrepancies that seem to unfold. The theoretical statement that arises out of such a reading, as oblique and self-negating as it may have to be, may violate the conventional notions of the literary text, the critical text, and the basis for their distinction, but violates them with rigor. Benjamin, like others before him, dissolves an old genre (literery criticism) in order to found a new genre that combines fiction and commentary in one.

*   *   *

Benjamin signals the difficulties of writing oneself into his logic. At the beginning of Part II of the essay, in what seems like a casual observation about everyday life, he writes: "The most important thing one has to say is not always proclaimed aloud. And even secretly it is not always confided to those most intimate and closest to us" (p. 359). This reflection on life serves also as an indication for the interpretation of Benjamin's own text: it does not always say openly what it has to say, not even to the person closest to it, the reader of the text.

One already senses this opaqueness in the title "Zum Bilde Prousts."[2] Does the essay present a portrait of the man Proust or is it rather a discussion of the literary image, a consideration of the Proustian metaphor? Benjamin's text authorizes no clear choice. On the one hand, it speaks of Proust's life, his desire for happiness, of his homesickness, his curiosity, his relationship to society, his death. On the other, it speaks of the writing of Proust's "woven" text, of his "cult of resemblance," or of the articulation of his sentences. The biographical portrait is so interwoven with textual considerations about the imagery that no single interpretation of the title seems unambiguously privileged.

Benjamin gives an explicit definition of the term "Bild," but it appears in a code language that cannot be learned, except (perhaps) in the course of his essay: "The image [*Bild*] of Proust is the highest physiognomic expression that the incessantly growing discrepancy between poetry and life was able to produce" (p. 355). In Benjamin's definition the image is neither the image of life nor the image of poetry, but rather that which marks the ever-increasing discrepancy between the two. "This is the moral," Benjamin continues, "which justifies the attempt to call it [the image] up" (p. 355). And the essay

"Zum Bilde Prousts" is just this attempt—to call up the image, much as one would call an actor before the stage-curtain in the attempt to distinguish him, if only for a moment, from his former fictitious role.

The ambiguous relationship between life and poetry, which underlies the definition of the Proustian image, becomes the fundamental if veiled concern of the entire essay. What is ultimately thematized by virtue of the imposed discrepant interpretations of the term *"Bild"* is neither Proust's life nor his literary imagery, but rather the relationship between life and image and what this relation implies about the possibility of interpretative judgment.

*   *   *

Benjamin refers to Proust's image as an expression of discrepancy between life and poetry; and immediately following this description, he begins to elaborate this relationship. In an intricate, repeatedly self-questioning paragraph that attempts to characterize Proust's *À la recherche du temps perdu*, Benjamin traces a movement between these two extremes, a movement that begins in life and finally leads to the purely ornamental work of poetry. These characterizations involve a particular concept of life and memory in which life seems to assert an original priority over the fictional text and in which memory serves as an access to that life. But each new sentence progressively distances itself from this concept, until life and memory are replaced by a woven (textual) work of forgetting.

> Man weiß, daß Proust nicht ein Leben, wie es gewesen ist, in seinem Werke beschrieben hat, sondern ein Leben, so wie der, der's erlebt hat, dieses Leben erinnert. Und doch ist auch das noch unscharf und bei weitem zu grob gesagt. Denn hier spielt für den erinnernden Autor die Hauptrolle gar nicht, was er erlebt hat, sondern das Weben seiner Erinnerung, die Penelopearbeit des Eingedenkens. Oder sollte man nicht besser von einem Penelopewerk des Vergessens reden? Steht nicht das ungewollte Eingedenken, Prousts *mémoire involontaire* dem Vergessen viel näher als dem, was meist Erinnerung gennant wird? (pp. 355–56)

It is known that Proust did not describe a life as it was in his work, but rather a life in the way that he who experienced it remembers this life. And yet even that is still imprecise and far too clumsily said. For here it is not what he experienced that plays the main role for the remembering author, but rather the weaving of his remembrance [*Erinnerung*], the Penelope work of memory [*Eingedenken*]. Or shouldn't one rather speak of a Penelope work of forgetting. Isn't the involuntary memory, Proust's *mémoire involontaire*, much closer to forgetting than to that which is usually called remembrance?

Benjamin begins in the sure tone of one who is well beyond obvious mystifications about the nature of this "auto-biographical work" (p. 355). It is common knowledge that Proust relates life as he remembers it and not life as it really was. Yet the tone of surety rapidly gives way: Benjamin shuttles back and forth between possibilities and each new attempt at characterization puts its predecessor into question. The novel is not memory of lived experience, but rather the interweavings of memory, a "Penelope work of memory." Life no longer plays a role here, although the notion of "memory" still echoes a fragile link to experience. But Benjamin promptly breaks this link: Proust's novel would more aptly be called a "Penelope work of forgetting." The passage begins by describing the literary work as the plenitude of life to which memory gives access, but its final description is the farthest possible from life and memory—the woven work of voided life, forgetting.

As the paragraph continues, it is as though the trajectory from memory of life to the woven poetical text of forgetting cannot be quite completed, as though in describing the literary work one is forced to fall back upon a description into which life once again enters.

> Und ist dies Werk spontanen Eingedenkens, in dem Erinnerung der Einschlag und Vergessen der Zettel ist, nicht vielmehr ein Gegenstück zum Werk der Penelope als sein Ebenbild? Denn hier löst der Tag auf, was die Nacht wirkte. An jedem Morgen halten wir, erwacht, meist schwach und lose, nur an ein paar Fransen den Teppich des gelebten Daseins, wie Vergessen ihn in uns gewoben hat, in Händen. (p. 356)

Instead of a "Penelope work of forgetting" in which memory has no place, we have an interweaving of the two. Memory directs itself toward an attainable end (it is "goal-linked") and belongs to the daytime of lived experience, to the goal-bound actions of life. Forgetting, on the other hand, unlinked to any goal, is purely "ornament": it belongs to the night in which the patterned carpet of what seems to be lived experience is woven. The inter-play between them is such that the life-linked utilitarian memory seems repeatedly to unravel the textured ornamentation that forgetting has woven. "Each day, with its

---

And isn't this work of spontaneous memory, in which remembrance is the woof and forgetting the warp, rather a counterpart to the work of Penelope than its likeness? For here the day unravels what the night wove. Every morning, awakened, we hold in our hands, mostly weakly and loosely, only by a couple of fringes, the tapestry of lived experience, as forgetting wove it in us.

goal-bound action and, even more, with its goal-linked remembering, unravels the weaving, the ornaments of forgetting" (p. 356). Yet by the end of the passage, day finally becomes transformed to night, and with it the apparent priority of memory over image or ornament becomes reversed.

> Darum hat Proust am Ende seine Tage zur Nacht gemacht, um im verdunkelten Zimmer bei künstlichem Lichte all seine Stunden ungestört dem Werk zu widmen, von verschlungenen Arabesken sich keine entgehen zu lassen. (p. 356)

The life-bound remembrance of the daytime gives way to forgetting, to the artificial and purely ornamental work of the night. The second part of the paragraph retraces the movement away from life and memory toward poetry: in the interplay between the apparently privileged "remembrance" and its counterpart, "forgetting," it is the ornaments of forgetting that win out. The passage marks the same discrepancy that earlier defined the image (p. 91).

*   *   *

These same patterns repeat themselves throughout Benjamin's essay. Where a passage seems to concern Proust's life, one finds in the last analysis a becoming ornament of memory, a becoming metaphor of remembrance. The long paragraph that closes Part I of the essay, for example, speaks of Proust's "elegiac concept of happiness," in which memory provides access to the past and enables identity or coincidence with an origin. Here one finds "the eternal once-again, the eternal restoration of the original, first happiness. It is . . . this elegiac concept of happiness that transforms existence into a forest perserve of memory for Proust" (p. 357).

Benjamin suggests that this same desire for a restoration of the past functions not only in Proust's personal life but also in the literary work, where such nostalgic longings seem to be satisfied by that concept of memory so central to the novel, the *mémoire involontaire*. The *mémoire involontaire* is brought into play by citing Max Unold's commentary on the well-known madeleine passage: in his interpretation Unold emphasizes the complete success of the episode to carry one

---

Therefore, in the end, Proust transformed his days to night, in order, in the darkened room with artificial light, to devote all his hours undisturbed to the work, to allow none of the intertwined arabesques to escape him.

from the present moment to a realm of dream. But here a confusing and unsettling disparity becomes evident. The *mémoire involontaire* that transports the reader away from the present differs entirely from the notion of memory first described as satisfying the elegiac desire for perfect coincidence with a past. While insisting on the dream as the key to an interpretation of Proust, Benjamin describes this dreamworld as precisely that realm in which coincidence is absent, for things are merely similar here but never identical.

> An ihn [den Traum] muß jede synthetische Interpretation von Proust anschließen.... Das ist Prousts frenetisches Studium, sein passionierter Kultus der Ähnlichkeit.... Die Ähnlichkeit des Einen mit dem Andern, mit der wir rechnen, die im Wachen uns beschäftigt, umspielt nur die tiefere der Traumwelt, in der, was vorgeht, nie identisch, sondern ähnlich ... auftaucht. (p. 358)

This fundamental disparity that characterizes the dream as a realm devoid of an apparent plenitude is further elaborated in an oddly pedestrian image. To show how this marking of nonidentity takes place, Benjamin offers us a sign (*Wahrzeichen*), of this world, a rolled-up stocking.

> Kinder kennen ein Wahrzeichen dieser Welt, den Strumpf, der die Struktur der Traumwelt hat, wenn er im Wäschekasten, eingerollt, "Tasche" und "Mitgebrachtes" zugleich ist. Und wie sie selbst sich nicht ersättigen können, dies beides: Tasche und was drin liegt, mit einem Griff in etwas Drittes zu verwandeln: in den Strumpf.... (p. 358)

The stocking is rolled-up and thus gives the appearance of being filled. It seems to have an attainable contents, the outside of the stocking functioning both as container and as a sign of its contents. But when the children reach into the stocking, just when that which was formerly hidden (merely indicated) is about to become revealed and present, they discover that the stocking contains nothing but its

---

Every synthetic interpretation of Proust must connect to it [the dream].... That is Proust's frenetic study, his impassioned cult of similarity.... The similarity of one thing to another that we count on, that occupies us while awake, merely plays around the deeper similarity of the dreamworld in which what takes place never emerges as identical, but rather as similar.

Children know a sign of this world, the stocking, that has the structure of the dreamworld, when, rolled-up in the laundry chest, it is at the same time both "pouch" and "bundle" [*Mitgebrachtes*]. And just as they cannot sate themselves with transforming both of them, pouch and contents, with a grasp into a third thing—into the stocking....

rolled-up self. The apparent contents do not exist; the outside surface only seemed to assure access to a full interior. The rolled-up stocking that functions as a sign of its own fullness is now emptied of its apparent meaning: it has become an empty sign, signifying nothing beyond itself and serving no purpose. It is mere ornament. But the frivolous nature of the sign does not surprise the children. For them the reach into the stocking is a game. They know from the start that the apparent container is empty. It is not their desire for a content which they have difficulty satisfying: they are obsessed rather with the goalless desire to repeat the game of transforming pocket and contents into the stocking.

Benjamin introduces the stocking as a sign for Proust's dream-world: in what way then is the "structure" of the stocking in the laundry chest also that of the dreamworld reached by Proust's *mémoire involontaire*? Spontaneous remembrance at first seems very like that memory which satisfies an elegiac desire for coincidence with past happiness, but it brings us instead to a world of nonidentity. As the children play their game the rolled-up stocking seems, like the *mémoire involontaire,* to promise access to a plenitude behind it; but what seemed to function as a container and as a sign for a fullness is found to have always from the first been a mere stocking, an empty sign.

The children's play with the stocking is like a particular gesture of Proust's: just as the children cannot satiate their desire to transform the pouch and its contents into the stocking, "So Proust could not get his fill of emptying the dummy, the Self, with a grasp in order over and over to bring in that third thing—the image" (p. 358). The *Attrappe* (which may be translated as "dummy," "imitation," "trap") for which Proust reaches seems to signify the hidden presence of the self. But the grasp that should render this contents present only leads to a voiding of the self. The dummy that seemed to promise the plenitude to self was always a mere image, just as the full pocket of the children was always mere stocking. The gesture of Proust, like that of the children, is only a game. His insatiable desire is not the longing for the presence of the self, but rather simply the desire to repeat the movement, to transform the dummy over and over into the empty image.

Because of the structure of the comparisons, the relationship between the dream, the stocking and Proust's game is perplexing. The stocking is a sign for the dreamworld, and the gesture of Proust is in turn said to be "like" the children's game with the stocking. What relationship then is there between the unsuccessful grasp for the self

and an act of memory which leads to the dreamworld of noncoincidence? In this way the quest for the self is described not only in spatial
but also in temporal terms, as a returning to and reappropriating of
the past. Benjamin follows the movement of *À la recherche du temps
perdu* where Marcel attempts to make a lost self present to him by
recapturing past time. The quest for the self can only take place in this
futile attempt to render a past self present. Benjamin compares this
unsuccessful reappropriation to the emptying of an apparently full
sign in the children's game with the stocking. The sign functions as a
trap, as a feigned representation of a reality (of life) existing prior to it
and serving as its origin; it seems to promise access to that origin but
inevitably turns out to be empty. Memory, like language, seems to be
the trace of that which existed before and the promise of its reappropriation. But the movement of the *mémoire involontaire*, like that of
the sign, repeatedly marks the impossibility of this reappropriation.
That which we call the self was always mere figure, the "trap" which is
an apparent imitation but which cannot coincide with a former origin.

What is bewildering in Benjamin's comparisons of the dreamworld,
stocking, and dummy is their striking dissimilarities. If the game with
the stocking functions as a sign for the dreamworld, it is not because
their similarity is obvious, not because a stocking in a laundry chest is
an evident imitation or representation of a dreamworld. "The stocking," Benjamin writes, "has the structure of the dreamworld." The
structure of both the dreamworld and stocking is the feigned movement toward coincidence that leads to nonidentity: it is the structure
in which that which might seem to imitate successfully demonstrates
its own emptiness, its failure to give access to that which it represented. The similarity between the dreamworld and the stocking
(their structure) is that which states the impossibility of their similarity. The relationship established between the dreamworld and its sign
is one of noncorrespondence, of discrepancy. The dreamworld does
not serve as an origin to which its sign, the stocking, gives access.
Benjamin calls the stocking a sign, but chooses a term that avoids the
connotation of imitation: the stocking is a *Wahrzeichen*, a sign in the
sense of a token.

The construction of Benjamin's comparisons becomes somewhat
more comprehensible now. The stocking is like the dreamworld (it
serves as its sign), and Proust's game is in turn said simply to be "like"
that of the children. Benjamin refuses to specify whether Proust's
grasp for the self is an image of the dreamworld or the dreamworld

itself. He merely lists a series of elements and calls them similar, so that one is never quite sure which is a sign for which, which functions as a source and which as sign. There is merely a repetition without origin, a repetition that is never identity.

After this tangle of complexities, the paragraph seems to return to its original theme. It began with Proust's elegiac desire for a return to former happiness by way of memory. And as Part I of the essay closes, Benjamin writes once again biographically of the novelist's nostalgic desires; and yet this "homesickness" (*Heimweh*) is not quite the elegiac longing that could be stilled by a restoration of the past. It is stilled rather by the image that arises out of Proust's pretended grasp for the self: "The image ... stilled ... his homesickness. ... Torn by homesickness, he lay on his bed. Homesickness for the world distorted in the state of similarity" (pp. 358–59). We now know this world of similarity for which Proust yearned to be a world of nonidentity.[3] Everything that takes place in Proust belongs to this world of noncoincidence in which nothing more (and nothing less) happens than a repeated bringing forth of the image.

> Heimweh nach der im Stand der Ähnlichkeit entstellten Welt.... Ihr gehört an, was bei Proust geschieht, und wie behutsam und vornehm es auftaucht. Nämlich nie isoliert pathetisch und visionär, sondern angekündigt und vielfach gestützt eine gebrechliche kostbare Wirklichkeit tragend: das Bild. (pp. 358–59)

Proust's text may seem to grasp back toward life, toward a former self, but it performs this fictional gesture, this game, merely so that the image may emerge, in order to define the image once again by marking the discrepancy between life and the literary text.

This game that Benjamin describes as Proust's is similar to the game that he himself repeatedly plays. Benjamin speaks of Proust in the nostalgic tone of a memorist wishing to recall a lost acquaintance to life and in turn presents Proust's yearning as though it were an elegiac desire for childhood happiness: he offers these traps, these dummies of both his and Proust's nostalgia for past life in order to empty them, in order to let them emerge as empty sign—so that the image of his

---

Homesickness for the world distorted in the state of similarity. ... To it belongs what takes place in Proust—and how carefully and elegantly it arises. Namely, never isolatedly lofty and visionary, but rather heralded and multiply supported, bearing a fragile, precious reality—the image.

own writing may arise out of the discrepancy marked between life and literature. It rises up out of the articulation of Benjamin's sentences.

*   *   *

The path from the fullness of life to the image has become so familiar that its precipitousness no longer shocks us. We have retraced this trajectory five times in the first section of the essay. And it is through this repetition of similar gestures that we may claim comprehension of these passages, even though this understanding was originally based on a definition of the image which itself was apparently nonsensical—at best cryptical: "The image [*Bild*] of Proust is the highest physiognomic expression that the incessantly growing discrepancy between poetry and life was able to produce" (p. 355).

The manner in which interpretation depends on previous parts of the text becomes especially evident in the opening of the essay's third section. The passage is written in a code that can be deciphered and given full meaning only by reflecting on and reappropriating past language and structure. Benjamin describes Proust's notion of "eternity" with a peculiar spatial terminology: "The eternity that Proust opens to view is intertwined time, not limitless time. His true interest concerns the passage of time in its most real, that is its *space-crossed* figure" (p. 365, italics mine). We are given some indication of what this interweaving of time and space might suggest, when a terse parallel construction places remembrance in the role of time and aging in that of space: "the passage of time in its . . . space-crossed figure, which nowhere prevails in a more undisguised form than in remembrance, within, and in aging, without" (p. 365). The figure of time that concerns Proust is time intertwined with space or the interweaving of remembrance and aging.[4]

This passage reminds one of an earlier "intertwining" of remembrance and forgetting:[5] a counterplay arose between the two, in which the weaving of the purely ornamental tapestry of forgetting finally gained ascendancy over goal-bound remembrance. The new terminology that Benjamin now uses is the counterplay between remembrance and aging—and aging will be seen to play a very similar role to forgetting: like forgetting, aging records the image of lived life,[6] and like forgetting, it both gains ascendancy over its opposite and brings forth the ornament or image.

As Benjamin further develops the Proustian concept of time, he continues to speak a code language, *Schlüsselsprache* (p. 362), substantially dependent on earlier passages for its decoding. "Following the counterplay between aging and remembrance means penetrating to the heart of the Proustian world, to the universe of intertwining. It is the world in the state of similarity" (p. 365). Earlier Benjamin introduced this notion of similarity (*Ähnlichkeit*) and with elaborate care differentiated the everyday concept from similarity as it functions at the heart of Proust's dreamworld: that which is similar is that which is "never identical." And what takes place in this world of noncoincidence, the earlier passage also describes: to this realm belongs all that takes place in Proust—the bringing forth of the image.[7]

The puzzling formulation about the nature of Proustian eternity draws its meaning from the two passages previously interpreted, because the laws of remembrance are operative even within the confines of the essay. Remembering what took place when Benjamin first described the intertwining of memory and forgetting (here called memory and aging), and how he later showed the image arising from Proust's "world . . . in the state of similarity" (pp. 358–59), we may expect here in Section III, once again to experience the marking of discrepancy between life and poetry and the bringing forth of the *Bild* which has been so carefully heralded.

Just this process is elaborated by the second half of the passage.

> Das ist das Werk der mémoire involontaire, der verjüngenden Kraft, die dem unerbittlichen Altern gewachsen ist. Wo das Gewesene im taufrischen "Nu" sich spiegelt, rafft ein schmerzlicher Chok der Verjüngung es noch einmal so unaufhaltsam zusammen. . . . (p. 365)

The *mémoire involontaire* or rejuvenating force engages in continual and apparently successful counterplay with the relentless process of aging. The past mirrors itself in the present instant, and the recollection of one's youth is played out when the past becomes snatched up with a painful shock: this shock of rejuvenation brings about a reappropriation of the past.

Yet only a few lines later, Benjamin names this very process in which the past mirrors itself in the present not only rejuvenation but also "aging" or "decay" (*Altern*). "Proust performed the monstrous act of letting the entire world *age* by an entire human life in an instant" (p. 365, italics mine). The gesture that would seem to render one a lifetime younger brings loss of life instead: the concentration of past

---

That is the work of the *mémoire involontaire*, of the rejuvenating force, which is a match for relentless aging. When the past [*das Gewesene*] mirrors itself in the dew-fresh "instant," a painful shock of rejuvenation snatches it up once again as incessantly. . . .

and present which attempts a reappropriation of life (*Verjüngung*) brings about its instantaneous consumption. "Precisely this concentration, in which what otherwise simply wilts and dims consumes itself in a flash, is called rejuvenation [*Verjüngung*]" (p. 365).

Proust's grasp toward life—the attempt at rejuvenation through memory—brings aging much as in the earlier passages it brought forgetting (p. 356), the ornament (p. 356), or Proust's dreamworld of discrepancy (p. 358). We have come to expect this playful gesture that results in voided life, yet, as Benjamin goes on he seems to invert his description of the Proustian enterprise. "*À la recherche du temps perdu* is the unending attempt to charge an entire life with the highest presence of mind [*Geistesgegenwart*]. Not reflection [*Reflexion*]—bringing to mind [*Vergegenwärtigung*] is Proust's method" (p. 365). A terminology of presence apparently replaces that of decay (aging, wilting, dimming, consuming). Proust chooses to render present rather than merely to contemplate. And yet *Reflexion* and *Vergegenwärtigung* each permit another interpretation. Reflection or mirroring serves as the gesture for the renewal of lost fullness of life, ("When the past mirrors itself in the dew-fresh 'instant'") and *Vergegenwärtigung* may also indicate the realizing of an image. Benjamin's formulation may now be read as follows: Not the attempt to reappropriate the past by mirroring it in the present instant—but bringing in the image is Proust's artistic method. This is not to say that Proust simply chooses the image and rejects the attempts to reappropriate past life. His method is tracing the path from reflection—to the image. Benjamin carefully places a hyphen to indicate just this.

Earlier in the passage Benjamin described this same trajectory as passing from reflection (remembrance, rejuvenation) to aging. How then can aging and the recording of the image serve interchangeably to mark this end point?

> Er [Proust] ist ja von der Wahrheit durchdrungen, daß wir alle keine Zeit haben, die wahren Dramen des Daseins zu leben, das uns bestimmt ist. Das macht uns altern. Nichts andres. Die Runzeln und Falten im Gesicht, sie sind die Eintragungen der großen Leidenschaften, der Laster, der Erkenntnisse, die bei uns vorsprachen—doch wir, die Herrschaft, waren nicht zu Hause. (pp. 365–66)

He [Proust] is imbued with the truth that we all have no time to live the true dramas of existence that are allotted to us. That makes us age. Nothing else. The wrinkles and folds in our faces are the recordings [*Eintragungen*] of the great passions, of the vices, the knowledge [*Erkenntnisse*] that called on us—yet we, the masters, were not at home.

Proust understood that none of us has time to live the drama of his existence and that it is this incapacity for immediate experience that makes us age. The process of aging dictates the expressions of our physiognomies, etches our image,[8] the wrinkles and folds of the face: aging is the process that brings forth the image and marks the direction of the Proustian endeavor. This image of ourselves, although it records our lived lives, also indicates our absence in the face of that experience. Our passions and vices and even our knowledge come to us when the self is not at home: ". . . yet we, the masters, were not at home" (p. 365). Thus all remembrance of things past indicates the inevitable absence of the self from itself. As we pass from rejuvenation and remembrance of life to aging or the image, the "nicht zu Hause [Sein]" of the self becomes apparent and we realize the impossibility both of learning and experience (knowledge, passions, vices). Benjamin summarizes this succinctly in the second part of his essay: "Isn't the quintessence of experience [*Erfahrung*] to learn [*erfahren*] how very difficult it is to learn/experience [*erfahren*] many things" (p. 361).

We have finally been able to decipher all the terms of the enigmatic opening of Section III. The interweaving of remembrance and aging, the heart of Proust's world as the state of similarity, the shock of rejuvenation which is also aging, and the etching of the physiognomy—all these we seem to have filled with meaning. The attempt to reappropriate the past through memory results in aging rather than rejuvenation: aging brings forth the portrait-image that marks the impossibility of direct experience or genuine learning: that which once took place is never rendered present to us as unmediated truth, but merely as image.

Yet this very message which our interpretation brings forth, dramatizes a certain emptiness in the interpretative method imposed by the essay. In order to give meaning to an obscure and complex web of images, we were forced to re-collect earlier passages in which these terms and structures first appeared. We grasped back toward these (as toward a past life), investing them with the validity of truth, only to find that the message they enable us to construct is that these 'original' passages too were always mere metaphor. The sole meaning at which the interpretation can arrive is the pure metaphoricity of its own language.

* * *

If we look over the three passages thus far read, we find each relating a different version of the same story—the story of the becoming-image of memory of life. At the outset of each of these passages, memory seems to promise access to experienced life or to the self, it seems to create a continuum in which reflection may bring about a coincidence of past and present. Memory plays this role, however, with no other purpose than to reveal its fictionality, for it inevitably serves as a bridge to the image rather than to life. And yet such theatrics to bring in the image are not entirely arbitrary. The image can never be presented—except as a relationship between particular images. The image, Benjamin writes, is a frail reality (p. 359) that emerges from the articulation of the Proustian sentences. It emerges out of a relationship which is also a movement, that is, out of the fiction of its own creation from memory, from life, from the self. The image comes forth as this fictional path becomes marked *as* fiction, as the text which points to its origins is shown always to have been image.[9]

Repeating Benjamin's definition of the image, we find that its terms have been rendered less opaque through their relationship to other passages of the essay. "The image [*Bild*] of Proust is the highest physiognomic expression that the incessantly growing discrepancy between poetry and life was able to produce." That discrepancy characterizes the relationship between life and poetry is the recurrent experience of Benjamin's essay. Every time this poetry (for Benjamin's is also a literary text) attempts to speak of (Proust's) life, one finds a transformation into the image. Benjamin repeatedly thematizes this movement of his own writing, for example in the becoming-stocking of that which seems to be a pouch filled with a contents or in the becoming-image of Proust's dummy self. Benjamin's language, which pretends to be *memoire* language, which seems to speak of life, states the fictionality of its apparent endeavor by showing the coincidence of poetry and life to be impossible.

The naming of the image as a "physiognomic expression" has become less enigmatic than at first. At first glance, perhaps, nothing seems less likely to mark a discrepancy between life and that which names it: a facial expression, being rather the most unequivocal sign of a particular human existence, seems to place itself definitively at the pole of life. Yet the physiognomy has served twice in the course of Benjamin's essay as a metaphor for the image,[10] that is as a metaphor for the absence or forgetting of life rather than for its presence. And it is solely by virtue of this repetition that the reader learns to invert the "meaning" of the facial expression. Benjamin names the image a "physiognomic expression" because the violence thus done to this expression, which robs it of its potentiality to provide immediate access to life, is that which all language has undergone—and is that which defines the image.

Still problematic in the definition is why the discrepancy between life and poetry is said to be "incessantly increasing." The gap between life and literary language could be maintained as constant only if the two poles of the trajectory could be definitively determined. Yet this proves possible for neither life nor the image. Life is continually experienced as already in the process of being voided. And the "image" which is named as the other end point of the trajectory can only be regarded as a metaphor for itself. The image arises out of the discrepancy between life and the language that names life (whether it be called "ornament," "image," or "physiognomy"): the path between the two poles is traversed only at the price of learning that that which the image names is absent.[11] The very 'presence' of the so-called image at the end of the trajectory indicates the absence of that which it names—itself.[12]

Neither the image nor life is ever rendered present as a definite terminus.[13] Nevertheless, Proust repeatedly traces (as does Benjamin) the path between these illusory vanishing points. Each reach toward life, each new pose of language as representational, takes place with an ever-increasing history of similar gestures before it, and therefore with a growing cognizance of the game-quality of the gesture that widens the gap between the two elusive poles.

How successful then is the critic's attempt to call up the image that Benjamin suggests as the very purpose of his text. "This is the moral that justifies the attempt to call it [the image] up" (p. 355). The attempt to call up figural language from the depths of its textual milieu, to isolate it in order to contemplate it as pure image, proves impossible: the image emerges from a movement of discrepancy and never presents itself directly as the object of experience.

* * *

If we read a fourth passage—that which closes the essay—we find that rather than deepening our knowledge of the Proustian world, it merely brings in another version of a now familiar story. The passage elaborates the symbiotic relationship between Proust's fatal illness and his creation. For this suffering affected not only Proust's daily life, but his art as well: "This asthma entered his art" (p. 368). Just how this threat of death entered Proust's art, Benjamin goes on to describe. The syntax of Proust's sentences revealed the fear of choking, a choking which could paralyze the rhythm of the breathing that constituted Proust's art: the inhalation of life to reappropriate past memories and the exhalation of memory through reflection on, or writing about, the past:

> Seine Syntax bildet rhythmisch auf Schritt und Tritt diese seine Erstick-ungsangst nach. Und seine ironische, philosophische, didaktische Re-flexion ist allemal das Aufatmen, mit welchem der Albdruck der Erin-nerungen ihm vom Herzen fällt. In größerem Maßstab ist aber der Tod, den er unablässig, und am meisten, wenn er schrieb, gegenwärtig hatte, die drohende erstickende Krise. (p. 368)

It is by no means clear that Proust's asthma simply entered his writing by threatening the artist with physical death and his work therefore with cessation. There is an alternative which Benjamin offers—by way of an offhand comment—to describe the relationship between this threat of death and Proust's art: "This asthma entered his art, *if indeed his art did not create it*" (p. 368, italics mine). That the threat of death should come from within Proust's own art rather than from the outside, that his text creates the very basis for its own paralysis will be seen to be the only explanation for the passage that follows.

> On a larger scale, death, which he incessantly had present to him, and most of all when he wrote, was the menacing crisis. In this way it faced Proust, and long before his malady took on a critical form. However not as a hypochondriac fantasy but rather as a *"réalité nouvelle,"* that new reality whose reflection on things and men are the traits of aging. (p. 368)

There can be no mistake that death, this "new reality" which turns all reflexion into the traits of aging, is, according to Benjamin's own code language, the image.[14] Proust's art has indeed produced the fatal disease: it is the image, Proust's own creation, that threatens to put an end to the apparently unproblematical respiration of Proust's novel.

His syntax imitates rhythmically, step by step, his fear of suffocation. And his ironical, philosophical, didactic reflection is always the breath with which the nightmare of remembrances falls from his bosom. On a larger scale, death, which he incessantly had present to him, and most of all when he wrote, is the menacing crisis.

The image, as we have learned from earlier passages, always brings about a voiding of life. This explains how death could have stood facing Proust long before his physical disease became critical and why it was present to him most especially when he wrote. The image threatens the respiration of the text because as the image arises it proves the fictionality of inhaling life to recapture memory and exhaling memory to form autobiography: the image arises out of a trajectory that denies reflection and memory as the origin of art.

Benjamin proposes to bring his reader to the very heart of this Proustian creation he has just described by means of "physiological stylistics" (p. 368). Bizarre as this may appear as a critical methodology, the term simply indicates the continuation of the physiological pattern of imagery already established by the passage: Proust's creation was said to take place in the face of death and to bring forth the physiognomy that marks the process of aging, and the workings of the *mémoire involontaire* were elaborated in terms of breathing. Benjamin continues to describe this Proustian memory as a kind of respiration. By following this process of respiration we are to arrive at the very core of the Proustian realm—presumably the original reality from which his text arose—and yet the path to this center proves somewhat encumbered:

> Physiologische Stilkunde würde ins Innerste dieses Schaffens führen. So wird niemand, der die besondere Zähigkeit kennt, mit der Erinnerungen im Geruchssinn (keineswegs Gerüche in der Erinnerungen) bewahrt werden, Prousts Empfindlichkeit gegenüber Gerüchen für Zufall erklären können. (p. 368)

The conventional notion of Proust's *mémoire involontaire* points to memory as that which preserves and gives access to the very reality from which the novel was elaborated; yet, according to Benjamin, it does not retain the scents of experience, does not store actual bits of the past. These memories can hardly be the life-source of Proust's work, since they appear as that which has already become image—as physiognomies (*Gesichtsbilder*) whose state of presence remains enigmatic if not incomprehensible.

Physiological stylistics would lead us to the innermost center of this creation. Thus no one who knows the peculiar tenacity with which remembrances are preserved in the sense of smell (by no means smells in remembrances) will be able to explain Proust's sensitivity to smells as accidental.

Gewiß treten die meisten Erinnerungen, nach denen wir forschen, als
Gesichtsbilder vor uns hin. Und auch die freischwebende Gebilde der
mémoire involontaire sind noch zum guten Teil isolierte, nur rätselhaft
präsente Gesichtsbilder. (p. 368)

And precisely because these memories are already images, in order
to penetrate to that which we may name the very deepest layer of
Proust's poetry, we must—all the while knowing that it is a mere
game—suggest to ourselves a time when memory was not yet image.

Eben darum aber hat man, um dem innersten Schwingen in dieser
Dichtung sich wissend anheimzugeben, in eine besondere und tiefste
Schicht dieses unwillkürlichen Eingedenkens sich zu versetzen, in
welcher die Momente der Erinnerung nicht mehr einzeln, als Bilder,
sondern bildlos und ungeformt, unbestimmt und gewichtig von einem
Ganzen so uns Kunde geben wie dem Fischer die Schwere des Netzes von
seinem Fang. (p. 368)

He who fishes in the sea of "lost time" in order to recapture past life
creates for himself this fiction of life-filled, pre-image depths into
which he can cast his net . And when he raises his catch to the surface,
it is only by way of his language ("his sentences") that he brings it
in—as images rather than life. What Proust brings forth through the
mémoire involontaire arises out of the articulation of his sentences, out
of that which is already image.

Der Geruch, das ist der Gewichtssinn dessen, der im Meere des Temps
perdu seine Netze auswirft. Und seine Sätze sind das ganze Muskelspiel
des intelligiblen Leibes, enthalten die ganze, die unsägliche Anstren-
gung, diesen Fang zu heben. (p. 368)

Certainly most of the remembrances we search for pass before us as physiognomies
[Gesichtsbilder]. And even the free-floating images [Gebilde] of the mémoire involontaire are
still for the most part isolated, only enigmatically present, physiognomies [Gesichtsbil-
der].

But precisely because of this, in order to knowingly give oneself to the innermost leap
[Schwingen] in this poetry, one must shift into a special, deepest stratum of this involuntary memory in which the moments of remembrance—no longer singly, as images
[Bilder], but rather void of images [bildlos] and formlessly, indeterminately and
weightily—proclaim themselves to us just as the weight of the net announces his catch to
the fisherman.

Smell, that is the sense of heaviness of he who throws out his nets in the sea of the temps
perdu. And his sentences are the whole play of muscle of the intelligible body, contain
the whole, the unspeakable strain to lift this catch.

Once again the text plays the game (*Muskelspiel*) of reaching for life through the *mémoire involontaire* in order to bring in the image. The catch that the sense of smell heralds is not the newly inhaled scents of experience, but memories which were already images. No life-preserving function of respiration takes place here, except that which the literary text itself creates as the fiction of its own imageless, non-metaphorical origin.

* * *

Benjamin ends his essay with just such a fiction of a moment when Proust's memories were not yet images. He describes the creation of Proust's novel in an ironical arabesque that masks itself as an apotheosis of art.

> Zum zweitenmal erhob sich ein Gerüst wie Michelangelos, auf dem der Künstler, das Haupt im Nacken, an die Decke der Sixtina die Schöpfung malte: das Krankenbett, auf welchem Marcel Proust die ungezählten Blätter, die er in der Luft mit seiner Handschrift bedeckte, der Schöpfung seines Mikrokosmos gewidmet hat. (p. 369)[15]

Proust's deathbed served, as did Michelangelo's scaffolding in the Sistine Chapel, as the uncomfortable structure on which, in spite of great suffering—and perhaps because of it—a momentous work was dedicated to the creation of life, to the origin of the world.

Benjamin may here extol the heroic dimensions of the Proustian creation, but this glorification follows immediately upon a warning against misinterpretation of the relationship between Proust's art and his suffering.

> Wie innig diese Symbiose dieses bestimmten Schaffens und dieses bestimmten Leidens gewesen ist, erweist am deutlichsten, daß nie bei Proust jenes heroische Dennoch zum Durchbruch kommt, mit dem sonst schöpferische Menschen sich gegen ihr Leiden aufheben. (p. 369)

For the second time a scaffolding arose like Michelangelo's, on which the artist, his head crooked backward, painted the Creation on the ceiling of the Sistine Chapel—the sickbed on which Marcel Proust devoted innumerable pages, that he covered in the air with his writing, to the creation of his microcosm.

Just how intimate this symbiosis between this particular creation and this particular suffering was, is shown most clearly by the fact that in Proust that heroic Nevertheless with which creative men otherwise raise themselves up [*sich aufheben*] against their suffering never bursts forth.

And another such warning appeared earlier in the essay:

> Proust selbst hat es ihnen [seinen Lesern] an vielen Stellen erleichtert,
> auch dieses oeuvre unter der altbewährten, bequemen Perspektive der
> Entsagung, des Heroismus, der Askese zu betrachten. (p. 357)

The relationship between Proust's creation and his suffering is not
literature arising from a melodramatic "Nevertheless" in the face of
extreme suffering. Proust's writings did not result from this life condition; rather it was his writings that created that condition, thus
producing the deadly disease that voids life and renders it image.

Benjamin says just this in his closing passage, albeit in his usual
oblique manner. Our previous readings put the excessive gravity of
these lines into its proper ironical perspective. As Proust lay on his
sickbed, we know now that it was no unifying life-source he yearned
for: he was torn apart by homesickness for a world of nonidentity, for
the realm of the image.[16] If this creation took place in the face of
death, it took place in the face of the *Bild* (for which death is a
metaphor,[17]) the image that indicates the fictionality of lived life.

And then again Proust's creation is not quite identical to
Michelangelo's paintings of the creation to which it is compared. The
Sistine Chapel paintings present the creation of life as the originary
moment of the world. But the origin to which Proust's novel refers is
not life, but the creation of the novel itself. Proust devoted his pages
to "the creation of his microcosm" (p. 369); that is, the very subject
matter of the novel is its own origin. The novel elaborates the fiction
of its own source, in a life preceding the text from which the image
pretends to arise: it does this in order to mark this origin as fiction, in
order to show that life was always a textual image. The text does not
arise from Proust's heroic life-will in the face of death, for it is the
textual image itself that is the very source of voided life.

*   *   *

What Benjamin indicates about [Proust's] literary work is its necessary camouflage as referential language. It apparently provides access
to life, to a self existing outside and prior to the text: it offers a

---

Proust himself made it easy for them [his readers] in many places to regard even this
oeuvre in the long standing, comfortable perspective of renunciation, heroism, asceti-
cism.

plenitude of language which provides a link to a realm external to itself. This feint is intrinsic to the text of fiction, to the text that invariably pretends to be that which it is not. But it is through this assumed role as literal language that the literary work indicates its fictionality. Not that language ever directly presents itself as metaphor (*Bild*), but it traces the discrepancy between itself and the life it pretends to name: this discrepancy marks the fictionality of its representational stance.

Just as literary language indicates its own figural nature, so Benjamin's essay camouflages itself as a language of plenitude and in the course of this dissimulation displays its own metaphorical nature. "Towards the Image of Proust," in pretending to read Proust's work as signifying a life which preceded it, assumes for itself the role of a language of truth, that is of a language which stands in relation to its object (Proust's novel, the society, thought, and author behind it), much as Proust's novel apparently did to its object. But as Benjamin's "critical" essay indicates the purely figural nature of the literary text, it also marks the fictionality of its own language. The name Proust and the object *À la recherche du temps perdu* are metaphors in the fiction entitled "Towards the Image of Proust." With the same movement that gives rise to the Proustian metaphor, in tracing the discrepancy between poetry and life, Benjamin indicates the relationship between the critical work and its object. The attempt to penetrate to the heart of the Proustian world, to move toward a coincidence with the literary work, is repeatedly followed by a return to the surface, by the marking of the discrepancy between the critical essay and its object. Benjamin's essay indicates the impossibility of its own discursive statement.

The complex strategy of Benjamin's text in its relationship to *À la recherche du temps perdu* is exemplary. Despite the peculiar theatrical gestures by means of which it chooses to speak of Proust, it nonetheless manages to make general commentary on the relationship between critical and literary texts. Most obviously, it presents an ironical commentary on the criticism which, through the literary work, claims to dis-cover the life (biography, society, psychology) that stands behind it; but Benjamin's essay is no less a commentary on criticism that pretends to be above any mystification about the metaphorical nature of language, which directly advances a concept of language as empty sign and develops these conclusions out of a purely intrinsic literary interpretation. For this criticism that claims to announce the eclipse of meaning in the literary text does so while in the same breath admit-

ting that this announcement was already in its literary object. It further risks displaying the emptiness of its own literal pretensions by
unavoidably calling attention to the relevance of this theory of nonreferential sign to its own text. This text, for example, adds nothing to
Benjamin's. It cannot claim to deconstruct "Towards the Image of
Proust" by revealing the essay's blindness to its own self-contradiction,
because the obliqueness of Benjamin's self-commentary is built into
the text's metaphorical nature: the language of the essay is fiction, so
that our text merely renders discursive that which was shown to be
necessarily oblique. If, as Benjamin's essay indicates, a text is forced to
comment on its own fictionality indirectly, there is no sure way to
distinguish between unintentional self-mystification and an intended
strategy of self-camouflage. The signs of the literary text not only
necessarily offer an apparent plenitude, but repeatedly perform the
text's demystification, deconstruct themselves. All intrinsic criticism is
already within the literary work, yet never appears in the language of
traditional commentary, but rather as a discrepancy indicated by a
language of fiction. There is a necessary disjunction in the voice of the
text, an ambivalence that marks the discrepancy between that which
its seems to say and that which it does not and therefore can say. The
text—though neither discursively nor definitively—traces the movement from full sign to empty sign.

AFTERWORD

"I, the Juggler"

CHAPTER FIVE

> juggle *vb* jug-gling [*ME* jogelen, *fr. MF* jogler
> *to joke, fr. L* joculari, *fr.* joculus, *dim. of jocus,*
> *joke*]
>
> *vi*   1: *to perform the tricks of a juggler*
>   2: *to engage in manipulation esp. to achieve*
>   *a desired end*
> *vt* 1a: *to practice deceit or trickery on: BE-*
>   *GUILE*
>   b: *to manipulate esp. to achieve a desired*
>   *end*
>   2a: *to toss in the manner of a juggler*
>   b: *to hold or balance insecurely*[1]

A fable began this text and it is surely now a fable that can best be manipulated to achieve its desired end. I tell a story told by Benjamin, who, he writes, heard it from Rastelli: "Rastelli narrates. . . ."[2] It is the tale of a renowned juggler who bears no name but that of the "master," who makes a journey from the west to the orient and from a certainty in the manipulation of his art to a certain insecurity in his own balance.

The "master" goes to Constantinople to juggle before another master—Mohammed Ali Bei, sultan of all the Turks. Ali Bei rules with the capricious inhumanity of a despot and the performance before him is the scene of an enormous risk. The nature of this risk may be read in his name, an almost-homonym of alibi, of being elsewhere, for the juggler is threatened with a nearly imperceptible displacement from his center of equilibrium, as imperceptible as the shift from Ali Bei to alibi.

And yet, it would seem, the threatened violence does not take place (unless by a sleight of hand not open to our perception), for the "master" serves that other master well, and his act meets with manifest admiration and loud acclaim. The secret of this wondrous skill is one who, in turn serves *his* "master" well. At the center of a large ball, the only property, sits the assistant, a dwarf, who "knew how to coincide with every impulse and every movement of his master." He follows the beat and obeys the trills of the flute, 'plays around,' indeed 'fawns around' his master, turning about the dancer like the earth around the sun.

The exorbitant path of the ball defies the laws of nature, giving the illusion of a virtuosity not to be comprehended by the human intellect. The "master" is, through his assistant, in control of this illusion, for his talent is, after all, merely an elaborate deception. Or is it? For when, the performance having ended, the "master" goes to meet his loyal servant, he finds instead a messenger from the dwarf. Having searched everywhere for him, he can now deliver the following letter: "'Dear Master, you must not be annoyed with me. . . . Today you cannot show yourself to the sultan. I am sick and cannot leave my bed.'– – –"

How is this to be interpreted? for Rastelli ends his story here. Certainly the shock of the letter's contents must—at least momentarily—throw the "master" off balance. The performance which he thought to take place through carefully planned artifice demonstrated a real virtuosity that before seemed only illusory. The juggler is indeed so perfect a manipulator of the ball that he is able to do the greatest violence to those laws known to determine its movement and still maintain his mastery.

A tale, then, of exemplary manipulation achieved only through violation of the law. Needless to say—for the title of this Afterword implies it—the "master's" relationship to the ball is an allegory of the relationship of a certain kind of interpretation to the literary text, an interpretation which, by violating the laws of the text, achieves such extraordinary control that it may even go beyond its dependence on the text/dwarf/ball and perform with an elaborate, self-sufficient virtuosity of its own.

$$* \quad * \quad * \quad * \quad *$$

Is this perfection of the "master" really the *only* interpretation of the story? Several questions remain unanswered. Why does Rastelli pause at the end of his narration, a pause significantly marked by "– – –." What does Rastelli's enigmatic commentary mean? "You see, added Rastelli, after a pause, that our profession wasn't born yesterday and that we have our own story—or at least our stories." Why a multiplicity of stories when he has apparently told but one? In the name of what profession does Rastelli speak? In other words—where's the "joke" or who's the "joker"[3] (the etymological roots of juggle and juggler).

A series of questions that hardly seem serious. "But for those dedicated by profession to the comical, serious things have a fatal attraction." This shift from the comic to the serious, taken from a prose poem of Baudelaire, is, perhaps, the answer to our dilemma. For that text, "A Heroic Death,"[4] with a story line very similar to "Rastelli narrates..." and often couched in almost identical terms, is played upon deliberately by Benjamin—translator of Baudelaire (over a period of nine years).

The obvious discrepancies between the two are at least as significant as their similarities. In Baudelaire's text, the jester has plotted to depose his prince, who, through an artistic ruse, then strikes the buffoon dead in the midst of his most accomplished performance. But are these really only discrepancies? In "Rastelli narrates...," the juggler's intention is to win over the sultan and, in a sense, to reverse their relationship of master/servant, to seize his sovereign authority. The "master" assumes for himself the powers of Ali Bei, the powers that formerly seemed alibi—elsewhere; which are, also, those of the dwarf. In terms of the allegory, the interpreter has won complete command over the text.

And yet there are certain (in light of the outcome apparently purely ornamental) arabesques in the description of the performance that seem to deny this perfect mastery. If the "master" is a musician, so is his dwarf: "he played on the compression springs that were located in the interior of the ball, as easily as on the strings of a guitar." If the "master" is a dancer, so is the ball: "the ball turned around the dancer and yet also didn't forget its own dance." In fact, the ball appropriates the body of the juggler as its playground and as its ground for play: "From head to foot there was no spot over which the ball did not play, and each spot, as it fled past, became its own playground." Could it be that the juggler is juggled? In Baudelaire's text, the prince commissions a child page to perform the final trick: could it be in Benjamin's text that the Ali Bei/alibi (prince and child) also play a final ruse? On accepting the dwarf's alibi that he was elsewhere, in his sickbed, the juggler is able to center all authority within himself. Yet what if the alibi was not true? for the dwarf is a joker. He was, of course, this day, as on all others, within the ball.

The dwarf, like the literary work, writes a supplementary text, a commentary on his own performance. The contents of this commentary ensnare the juggler in the fiction of his own virtuosity, for this is the moment in which the "master"-interpreter becomes convinced of his own mastery: yet it is also the moment when he falls into the most literal and naive interpretation.[5] The juggler takes the alibi at its word, believes the dwarf truly to have been elsewhere, forgetting just then that it is in the nature of the text to displace its meaning (elsewhere) from its apparent contents. The alibi tells a multiplicity of stories and misleads the "master," who, invariably, misses the joke.

This is why, when Rastelli narrates, he speaks less in the voice of the juggler than in that of the storyteller.

APPENDIX

A Translation of Walter Benjamin's:
"Rastelli narrates . . ."

This story I heard from Rastelli, the incomparable, unforgotten juggler, who told it one evening in his dressing room.

Once upon a time, he began, in ancient times, there was a great juggler. His fame had spread with the caravans and merchant ships far over the terrestrial globe, and one day even Mohammed Ali Bei, who then ruled over the Turks, learned of him. He sent off his messengers to the four directions of the wind with the task of inviting the master to Constantinople, so that in his own and imperial person he might convince himself of the master's artistic skill. Mohammed Ali Bei is reputed to have been a dictatorial, even inhumane, prince, and people said of him that at a sign from the prince, a singer who had sought a hearing but had not found approval was thrown into the deepest dungeon. But his generosity was also well known, and an artist who pleased him could count on a high reward.

After several months the master entered the city of Constantinople. He did not, however, come alone, even if he made very little fuss about his companion. And yet, by means of him he had been able to gain special honor at the sultan's court. Everyone knows that the despots of the orient had a weakness for dwarfs. And the companion of the master was indeed a dwarf, or, more precisely, a boy dwarf. And, to be sure, such an exceptionally fine, such a graceful and swift little creature that the likes of him had certainly never been seen at the sultan's court. The master kept his dwarf hidden, and he had his good reason for it. He worked that is a little bit differently from his colleagues. They, as is well known, went to the Chinese school and there

Translated from Walter Benjamin, *Gesammelte Schriften*, Band IV–2, Copyright © 1972 (Tübingen: Suhrkamp, 1972), "Rastelli erzählt . . .," pp. 777–80.

they became acquainted with sticks and plates, swords and fire-
brands. Our master, however, did not seek his honor in the quantity
and diversity of props, but stuck to a single one, which, in addition,
was the simplest and attracted attention only because of its unusual
size. It was a ball. The ball had brought him his world-wide fame and,
in fact, there was nothing that equaled the wonders that he performed with this ball. For those who had followed the game of the
master, it seemed as though he were dealing with a living, now docile,
now obstinate, now affectionate, now scoffing, now friendly, now neg-
ligent, comrade, and never as though he were dealing with a dead
thing. The two seemed used to one another, and, for better or worse,
totally incapable of coming out without one another. No one knew
about the secret of the ball. The dwarf, the nimble changeling, sat
inside. Through long years of practice, he knew how to coincide with
every impulse and every movement of his master, and he now played
on the compression springs that were located in the interior of the ball
as easily as on the strings of a guitar. In order to avoid all suspicion,
they never let themselves be seen side by side, and master and assistant never lived under the same roof during their travels.

The day commanded by the sultan had arrived. A stage framed by
curtains was erected in the hall of the half-moon which was filled with
the dignitaries of the ruler. The master bowed toward the throne and
brought a flute to his lips. After several preliminary runs, he went
over into a staccato to the beat of which the large ball approached
from the soffits. Suddenly, it had placed itself on its owner's
shoulder—not to leave him so soon again. It played around, it fawned
around its master. He had now put his flute away, and, as though he
knew nothing of his visitor, had begun with a slow dance that it would
have been a pleasure to follow if the ball hadn't captured all eyes. Just
as the earth turns around the sun and at the same time around itself,
so the ball turned around the dancer and yet also did not forget its
own dance. From head to foot there was no spot over which the ball
did not play, and each spot, as it fled past, became its own playground.
It occurred to no one to enquire about the music of this mute round
dance. For each caused the other to play—the master the ball and the
ball the master—just the way the small, concealed helper had found it
easy to do for years. So it remained for the longest time, until suddenly, with a whirl of the dancer, the ball, as if hurled away, rolled
toward the ramp, hit against it and remained hopping in front of it
while the master composed himself. Now the finale took place. Again

the master took hold of his flute. At first it was as though he wanted to accompany his ball more and more softly, whose jumps had become weaker and weaker. But then the flute seized the command for itself. The breath of the flutist became fuller, and, as though he were breathing new life into his ball in a new and powerful way, its jumps proved to be gradually higher, while the master began to raise his arm so that after he had calmly brought it to shoulder height he stretched out his little finger—always while playing music—onto which the ball, obeying a last, long trill, settled with a single bound.

A murmur of admiration went through the rows and the sultan himself began the applause. And the master gave a last demonstration of his art when he caught in flight the heavy, ducat-filled purse that was flung to him in answer to great demand.

A little later, he stepped out of the palace in order to await his loyal dwarf at a remote exit. There a messenger pushed his way through the guards to him. "I have looked for you everywhere, sir," he said to him. "But you left your quarters early and I was forbidden to enter the palace." With these words he brought forth a letter that bore the handwriting of the dwarf. "Dear Master, you must not be annoyed with me," it read. "Today you cannot show yourself to the sultan. I am sick and cannot leave my bed."– – –

You see, added Rastelli, after a pause, that our profession wasn't born yesterday and that we have our own story—or at least our stories.

NOTES

CHAPTER ONE—NIETZSCHE

1. It will perhaps seem paradoxical to consider a notebook of fragments a suitable unit for interpretation. And our method is even more questionable since, from the outset, we put together a history in order to camouflage this fragmentary nature. But the movement of this history will show itself to be a fragmentation that has nothing to do with the formal organization of the text into a series of numbered passages: it is a more radical fragmentation that takes place, and it takes place no less in those texts which present themselves as an organic whole—a fragmentation that shows the concept of a unified text to be illusion. We will therefore confirm Philippe Lacoue-Labarthe's suspicion that—perhaps, even *The Birth of Tragedy* indicates its inability to be a "book." "*The Birth of Tragedy* would still be, according to his hypothesis, a Book—despite the breaks, a certain trampling in place, and perhaps already a real inability to be one" ("Le détour," *Poétique* 5: 57). To this end, we will follow the same author's suggestion of reading its "own rough drafts" (ibid. p. 66).

2. In *The Birth of Tragedy* one reads: "For it is the fate of every myth to gradually crawl into the constriction of a supposedly historical reality." (*The Birth of Tragedy* I: 63). Since Nietzsche offers us the "historical reality," we must interpret it back to its mythical source. For an elegant elaboration of this, see Paul de Man's "Genesis and Genealogy in Nietzsche's *The Birth of Tragedy*," *Diacritics* (Winter, 1972): 44–53.

3. The passages cited here of the studies preliminary to *The Birth of Tragedy* are taken from the new Colli-Montinari edition: Friedrich Nietzsche, *Werke: Kritische Gesamtausgabe* (Berlin: Walter de Gruyter, 1978), Dritte Abteilung, Dritter Band. Each fragment is given a double designation, the number of the notebook, followed by the number of the fragment in brackets. All other citations are from the Schlechta edition (Munich, 1966). The roman numeral refers to the volume, the arabic numeral to the page. The translations are my own.

4. Cf. "Socrates was the element in tragedy, in music drama in general, that dissolved it" (1[15]): "Socratism is the uninterrupted celebration of the sacrifice of ancient tragedy" (3[6]).

5. Cf.

Tragedy—the chorus which, ecstatic, sees a vision, that spreads out before it totally *Apollonian*. (Italics mine, 8[46])

According to this knowledge, we have to understand Greek tragedy as the Dionysian chorus which discharges itself over and over again into an Apollonian world of images. (*The Birth of Tragedy* I: 52)

6. Cf. "The dithyramb... who sees the sufferings of individuation in the image: this image is also finally presented. The dramatic event is thought of only as vision. The music, dance, lyric is the Dionysian symbolism out of which the vision is born. Excitation of the basis of feeling into the projection of images." 8[7]

7. Although this actually describes the function of the image in Wagner, sufficient passages from *The Birth of Tragedy* itself would confirm such a reading of the relationship between image and music in general. Music bears the myth or image which in turn both speaks of the Dionysian and at the same time protects against it. Cf. *The Birth of Tragedy* I: 115, a passage cited in footnote 15 of this text, I: 92, a passage cited on p. 5 of this text and also:

> We looked at the drama and penetrated with a piercing glance into its inner, agitated world of motives, and yet it was as though only a simile passed us by, whose deepest meaning we almost thought we guessed and that we wished to tear away like a curtain in order to behold the originary image behind it. The brightest clarity of the image was not sufficient for us, for it seemed equally to reveal something and conceal it. And whereas its simile-like revelation seemed to call for the tearing of the veil, for the uncovering of its mysterious background, on the contrary, precisely that illuminated complete visibility held the eye entranced and prevented it from penetrating deeper. *(The Birth of Tragedy* I: 129)

8. Apparent opposites—since it is only through this false presentation of music as originary unity or as music without an inborn rupture, without the already inherent Apollonian, that music can appear as the clearly marked off contrary of the Apollonian.

9. Cf.

> Now beside this isolated knowledge as excess of honesty, if not presumption, stands a serious illusion which first appeared in the world in the person of Socrates—the unshakable belief that thinking, using causality as its guide, reaches into the deepest abysses of being, and that thinking is capable not only of knowing being but also of correcting it. *(The Birth of Tragedy* I: 84)

10. It is twice insisted here that the interpretation of the image by means of music brings us to the "myth." It is clear that myth may no longer be understood simply as the raising up of the Apollonian image—as I and Nietzsche until now seemed to imply. But an exact explanation of the term can only be attempted later.

11. The signifier *music*, therefore, is doubly inscribed (a game that is especially to be read in *The Birth of Tragedy*), once as the self-differentiating, as Will, and once again, subsequently, after the differentiation out of which the Apollonian arises—(if one could only speak meaningfully of an end point in this operation)—as music in the everyday, limited sense.

12. This multiple inscription of the "symbol" already contradicts its "conceptual" function.

13. Cf. Jacques Derrida's "Mythologie blanche," *Poétique* 5 (1971), especially pp. 6–8 and 44–45 concerning the "generalization of metaphoricity" in Nietzsche.

14. Cf. Maurice Blanchot, who describes the eternal return as a repetition that "turns aside," a repetition very similar to the inversion brought about by the symbol.

> L'éternel retour dit l'être du devenir, et la répétition le répète comme l'incessante cessation de l'être. L'éternel retour dit l'éternel retour du Même, et la répétition dit le détour où l'autre s'identifie au même pour devenir la non-identité du même et pour que le même devienne, en son retour qui le détourne, toujours autre que lui-même. L'éternel retour dit, parole étrangement, merveilleusement scandaleuse, l'éternelle répétition de l'unique, et elle la répète comme la répétition sans origine. *(L'entretien infini* [Paris: Gallimard, 1969], p. 238)

15. This deconstruction of the traditional theory of representation may be read more coherently in *The Birth of Tragedy* than in our own disconnected piecing together of fragments; more coherently, and yet these passages of discursive clarity are always inscribed in a questionable context.

> Tragedy places a lofty simile, the myth, between the universal validity of its music and the Dionysically receptive listener and awakens in him the illusion that music is merely the highest means of representation to enliven the plastic world of myth. Trusting in this noble deception, it may now move its limbs to the dithyrambic dances and give itself unhesitatingly to an orgiastic feeling of freedom, in which, without that deception, as music proper, it would not dare to revel. *(The Birth of Tragedy* I: 115)

The tragic myth is to be understood only as a symbolization of Dionysian wisdom through Apollonian artificial means: it [the myth] brings the world of appearance to its limits, where it denies itself and seeks to flee back to the womb of the true and only realities. *(The Birth of Tragedy* I: 121).

If one transfers now this phenomenon of the aesthetic spectator to an analogous process in the tragic artist, one will have understood the genesis of the *tragic myth.* It shares with the Apollonian art sphere the full pleasure in mere appearance and looking and at the same time denies this pleasure and has an even higher satisfaction from the destruction of the visible world of mere appearance. *(The Birth of Tragedy* I: 130)

16. We will later be able to establish the relationship between a speech that functions through the brevity and constriction of its expression and a certain kind of rhythm: they are both indicative of the stammer.

17. Nietzsche's text accomplishes what Michel Foucault so excellently terms "the genealogy of history" or "the real history" ("Nietzsche, la généalogie, l'histoire," *Hommage à Jean Hyppolite* [Paris: Presses Universitaires de France, 1971]). I, however, would not limit this "genealogy of history" historically (from 1874) as does Foucault. The deconstruction of history by means of a genealogical structure is already to be found at the beginning of Nietzsche's work and therefore contradicts the general tendency in Nietzsche interpretation to read the earliest texts as a naive origin.

18. Compare Gilles Deleuze:

Philosophos does not mean wiseman, but friend of wisdom. In what a strange manner must "friend" be interpreted: the friend says Zarathustra is always a third between I and me, that presses me to surmount myself and to be surmounted in order to live. The friend of wisdom is he who appeals to wisdom, but does so as one appeals to a mask in which one wouldn't survive—he who makes wisdom useful for new purposes, bizarre and dangerous ones, not very wise ones in truth. *(Nietzsche et la philosophie* [Paris: Presses Universitaires de France, 1970], p. 6)

19. The *perplexity* of the reader on which Nietzsche repeatedly insists is a sign of the reader's identification with the text as well as his differentiation from it. For "perplexity," true to its etymological roots (per—thoroughly, plectere—entwined), indicates his entanglement in the play, an entanglement which, on the other hand, shows itself to be the disparity of noncomprehension.

Nietzsche weaves the reader into the play within a play structure of *Hamlet*—as image of the hero—and with this gesture eliminates the last border between reality and illusion. For, however dizzying the play within a play of Shakespeare's tragedy may be, it seems to grant those who stand outside it—to the reason of the interpreting reader—a protective barrier, a *garde-fou.* Yet, according to Nietzsche's passage, identification with *Hamlet* violates the formerly safe, exterior border of the story and draws the reader, against his will, into the confusing game of masks.

This inscription into the game does not operate as the differentiation-less "inwardly warming understanding" that the reader has imagined. On the contrary. As the image of Hamlet, with each new reading, he hears his own voice as artificial, mediated, metaphor. For the rules of this game demand that the same be also the nonadequate, that an image may never coincide with its meaning.

The texts of those scenes alluded to in Nietzsche's fragment center precisely about the nonadequate nature of the image. Hamlet indeed recognizes the figure of his father, but will nevertheless continue to doubt whether it was the 'ghostly figure of a beloved dead one' or merely "intercourse with shadows." The doubtful nature of the image repeats itself at that moment when Hamlet attempts to make an image of this ghostly figure—to fix the metaphor in writing. It is by writing down the last words of the ghost that the hero swears to revenge the murder.

Remember thee!
Yea, from the table of my memory
I'll wipe away all trivial fond records,

All saws of books, all forms, all pressures past,
That youth and observation copied there;
And thy commandment all alone shall live
Within the book and volume of my brain.
............................[*Writing*]
    Now to my word;
It is 'Adieu, Adieu! remember me.'
I have sworn't.   (I, v: 98–112)

The last four acts demonstrate only the failure of this means of remembering the ghost (fixing its image): all is hesitation, doubt and illusion.

The second scene mentioned in which the reader identifies with Hamlet testifies even more directly to the nonadequate nature of the word. Hamlet—like the reader—enters with a book in hand. He plays the madman by using words such that they make sense and nonsense at the same time. His language operates on the border of reason, a language which, by comprehending all as metaphor, thus de-constructs its own reason.

Polonius: What do you read, my lord?
Hamlet: Words, words, words. (II, ii: 193–95)

20. That beat (*Takt*) is bound up with morality can be easily read out of the ambiguity of the word itself; *Takt* (tact) also as the fine sense of the correct.

21. Grimm: *Deutsches Wörterbuch* (Leipzig, 1960), X, 2, 1, p. 650.

22. *Der grosse Duden Herkunftswörterbuch* (Mannheim: Bibliographisches Institut, 1963), 7:668, 691.

23. To be sure, the word "stammer" does not actually appear in this passage, but in the first notebook of fragments there is a near repetition of the same: "The figures of Sophocles and Aeschylus are much deeper and greater than their words: they *stammer* beyond and about themselves." (Italics mine, 1[106].)

24. We read Nietzsche against Nietzsche: his "Self-Criticism" in any case considers *The Birth of Tragedy* as dialectical.

It smells offensively Hegelian.... An "idea"—the antithesis Dionysiac Apollonian—translated into metaphysics; history itself as the development of this "idea"; in tragedy the antithesis cancelled to become a unity. (*Ecce Homo* II: 1108)

In any case here spoke ... a *foreign* voice, the disciple of a still "unknown god," who hid himself for the time being under the hood of the scholar, under the gravity and dialectical aversion of the German. ("Attempt at Self-Criticism," *The Birth of Tragedy*, I: 12)

But the stammer proves to be anything but dialectic.

The thinking and reflecting of the hero is not Apollonian insight into his true essence, but rather an illusory stammering.... The dialectic errs. 9[28]

It does not preserve that which it reverses. It guarantees no meaning—rather, lack of knowledge.

25. This denial can hardly be considered a successful return to the original womb, although the phenomenon of Wagner seems to open itself to such an interpretation: for such a return bases itself on the possibility of history. The original Dionysian womb, the Originary One, was a necessary invention of the Socratic image of history. Compare *The Birth of Tragedy* I: 110, where a description of this return is subtly ironized (with expressions such as "seems," "analogically," "as if," "merely").

CHAPTER TWO—RILKE

1. The citations from Rilke's works are taken from *Sämtliche Werke* (Frankfurt: Insel-Verlag, 1966) and are referred to in the body of the text by volume (in Roman numerals) and page number (in Arabic numerals). Passages from the *Duino Elegies* (in Volume I) are referred to by verse number only. Translations are my own.

2. I owe this insight, as well as many others, to Paul de Man's essay prefatory to the recent French edition of Rilke: Rainer Maria Rilke, *Oeuvres,* ed. Paul de Man (Paris: Editions du Seuil, 1972).

> ... thought and poesy seem here to be indissolubly joined.
> For this reason even the best exegesis of Rilke is limited to a paraphrase, often very attentive and subtle, of the statement of the meaning. The interpreters do not place in question the convergence between the statement of the poems and the ontological status of the writing that constitutes them. (p. 12)

3. See, for example, the commentaries on the tenth elegy of J. F. Angelloz, *Les elegies de Duino* (Paris: Paul Hartmann, 1936), pp. 93-98; Franz Josef Brecht, *Schicksal und Auftrag des Menschen* (Munich: Ernst Reinhardt, 1949), pp. 256-75; Heinrich Cämmerer, *R. M. Rilkes Duineser Elegien* (Stuttgart: J. B. Metzlersche Verlagsbuchhandlung, 1937), pp. 132-44; Romano Guardini, *Rainer Maria Rilkes Deutung des Daseins* (Munich: Kösel-Verlag, 1961), pp. 367-419; Katarina Kippenberg, *Rainer Maria Rilkes Duineser Elegien und Sonette an Orpheus* (Wiesbaden: Insel-Verlag, 1948), pp. 113-21; and Heinrich Kreutz, *Rilkes Duineser Elegien* (Munich: C. H. Beck'sche Verlagsbuchhandlung, 1950), pp. 137-53. At once the most puzzling and predictable of these interpretations is that of Hans-Georg Gadamer, in "Mythopoietische Umkehrung in Rilkes Duineser Elegien" ["Mythopoeic Reversal in Rilke's Duino Elegies"], *Kleine Schriften II* (Tübingen: J. C. B. Mohr, 1967), pp. 194-209. Predictable because the hermeneutical task is defined as an explanation of the incomprehensible (p. 194), as a rendering coherent of the meaning of the whole (p. 195), and as a winning back of the meaningful and communicating text (p. 209). Yet this is a puzzling interpretation if ones takes the title of the essay at its word for the notion of textual *"Umkehrung"* hardly seems in complicity with paraphrase. Nevertheless, the reversal for Gadamer is reversible, and rather than suggesting the elusive nature of the text, only assures the possibility of making it present to us.

> ... that which has remained is the principle of poetic reversal. In Rilke it becomes mythopoeic reversal: the world of one's own heart is placed opposite us in the poetic legend as a mythical word, that is, as a world of acting beings. (p. 199)

> The hermeneutical conclusion is clear. The mythological phenomenon demands on its part a kind of hermeneutical reversal: the poetic assertion must be translated back. (p. 200)

> A translation back must always be possible that enables that which is present in the verses to be present to us. In this sense, Parousia is not only a theological concept, but also a hermeneutical one. Parousia means nothing other than Presence—and Presence by means of the word and only by means of the word and in the word, that is called a poem. (p. 209)

4. In the first *Duino Elegy,* Rilke writes:

> But the living all make
> the error, that they distinguish too sharply.
> Angels (they say) often do not know, whether they
> Walk among living or dead. (lines 80-83)

5. Cf. Jacques Derrida, "De l'économie restreinte à l'économie générale," in *L'écriture et la différence* (Paris: Editions du Seuil, 1967), pp. 369-407.

6. See pages 12-14 of de Man's essay, where he elaborates the implications of an apparently perfect coincidence between meaning and mode of discourse.

7. Certainly an eccentric use of language which I, however, justify with two definitions from *Webster's Seventh New Collegiate Dictionary.*

> 1. enclose, sheath
> 2. to fold in so that the outer becomes an inner surface.

The second reading sheaths the text with a new interpretation, superimposes a new surface that conceals the first. At the same time this new interpretation is not quite either the negation of the first nor a contradiction coming from the outside, rather a folding in of the first, leaving in its place a cleft which is not the same as an absence, but a play between its absence and its involuted presence. This invagination, this becoming-vagina is also something of a castration, only *something* of a castration, since it is questionable whether a phallus could ever have been present where there is now a vagina, and since the status of the phallus formerly present (in terms of the "originary suffering" and "originary-source") is doubtful anyway. These definitions are at best dizzying and at worst, perhaps, a bit fraudulent: I can only insist that the nature of this dizzying fraudulence will soon unfold.

8. It also places in question the conventional interpretation of "transformation" (*Verwandlung*) in Rilke (ninth Elegy).

9. Angelloz describes the young lamentation's function as that of attracting through her charms, and he attributes her inability to answer questions to her youth.

10. Rilke wrote a story with this same theme of the fallen aristocrat who nostalgically shows the ruins of his former castle—"Teufelspuk," IV: 574–81.

11. See Paul de Man:

> Nevertheless, in so far as it is desire for presence, lamentation almost inevitably transforms itself into the impatience of a desire that wishes to recuperate the missing entity. It tends to confer to the fictive world it constitutes a reality that it does not possess and seeks to appropriate it for itself as if it were an external reality. (p. 33)

See also, both p. 11 of the same essay and de Man's interpretation of "Orpheus Euridike Hermes" on pp. 32–33.

12. See the ninth Elegy, where Rilke speaks of the poetic enterprise as that of *Verwandlung*.

13. H. G. Gadamer does just this in "Mythopoietische Umkehrung in Rilkes Duineser Elegien." For him the *Gleichnis* will be the proof of the call to paraphrase in the opening lines.

> But precisely those who are so endlessly dead should "awaken an image" in us. That indicates expressly that there is something to be understood here. The long wandering of the complaint with the dead is not without sense and purpose. It leads to an insight and it is this insight towards which the entire poetic call of the elegies points: "that I some day, at the exit out of the violent insight, / Might sing jubilation and praise to assenting angels." (pp. 207–08)

14. It is Martin Heidegger who first elaborated on this relationship in Rilke between dangerous risk (*Wagnis*) and the image of the scale (*Waage*) in the texts "Wie die Natur die Wesen überläßt and "Wenn aus des Kaufmanns Hand" ("Wozu Dichter?," in *Holzwege* [Frankfurt: Vittorio Klostermann, 1963], pp. 248–95). While my interpretation owes much to Heidegger's, "Wozu Dichter" nevertheless wavers sometimes between the totality of the danger described and a certain security (well camouflaged as *Schutzlossein*) of presence and immanence (see, for example, pp. 286–87).

15. See also the early drama (1895) "Im Frühfrost," V: 707–73, and "Offener Brief an Maximillian Harden," V: 482–93 (1891).

16. Robert Graves, *The Greek Myths* (London: Penguin Books, 1969), II: 10.

17. Alfred Hermann explains this (away) as follows: "During Rilke's 1911 trip to Egypt, the animal body was stuck in the sand just as when Clara was there. Therefore the condition of the Sphinx image at that time is also the reason for the fact that Rilke's description and interpretation are limited to the kingly head." (*Rilkes Ägyptische Gesichte* [Darmstadt: Wissenschaftliche Buchgesellschaft, 1966], p. 425.)

18. See Jacob Steiner, *Rilkes Duineser Elegien* (Bern and Munich: Francke Verlag; 1962), p. 269.

19. This concealment is stressed in line 78 by the term *schweigend*.

20. Graves, op. cit., p. 10.

21. Riddle (as well as the German *Rätsel*) is etymologically linked to reading and interpretation. It is the powers of critical interpretation in fact which are at play. This game is precisely that of the text.

22. Cf. Guardini, p. 413: "In the spring, when the hazel is 'empty,' that is when it still has no leaves, it blooms but the blossoms—the masculine ones—do not rise up, but rather hang down."

23. "*asterisk* ... ; the character * used in printing or writing as a reference mark or an indication of the omission of letters or words" (*Webster's Seventh New Collegiate Dictionary*).

CHAPTER THREE—ARTAUD

1. All citations from *Héliogabale* and related texts are designated by a simple page reference and are taken from: Antonin Artaud, *Oeuvres complètes*, Vol. VII (Paris: Gallimard, 1967). Passages from *Le théâtre et son double* are marked *Théâtre*, followed by the page number, and are taken from Antonin Artaud, *Oeuvres complètes*, Vol. IV (Paris: Gallimard, 1964). Translations are my own. A shorter version of "The Assimilating Harmony" was first published in *Sub-Stance*, no. 17 (1977).

2. Letters presented as a supplementary explanation of the "Premier Manifeste" on the Theater of Cruelty.

3. See Jacques Derrida, "La clôture de la représentation," in *L'écriture et la différence* (Paris: Editions du Seuil, 1967), p. 350.

4. Cf. "Héliogabale, by sparing 'human' blood and without ever waging war, was able to practice a superior and philosophical idea of cruelty," p. 404.

5. A tendency of Jacques Henric, for example, in "Une profondeur matérielle," *Critique* (July 1970), pp. 616-26.

6. "This language—it can't be defined except by the possibilities of dynamic expression in space which are the opposite of possibilities of expression by means of the spoken word of dialogue" (*Théâtre*, pp. 106f.). See, also, *Théâtre*, p. 135.

7. Cf.

Now to change the destination of the word in the theater is to use it in a concrete and spatial sense . . . it's to manipulate it like a solid object that totters things. (*Théâtre*, p. 87)

. . . and it's at this level moreover that it [the word] acquires its major efficacy, like a dissociative force of material appearances, of all states in which the mind has stabilized itself and in which it would have a tendency to rest. (*Théâtre*, p. 84)

8. The human being, a sign or form that operates only in its relationship with other signs, loses his humanness.

You can see that these signs constitute veritable hieroglyphs, in which the human being, to the extent that he contributes to forming them, is nothing more than one form like another, to which he adds, however, a singular prestige as a result of his double nature. (*Théâtre*, p. 48, "La mise en scène de la métaphysique")

9. Cf.

We must note at the same time the hieroglyphic aspect of their costumes, in which the horizontal lines exceed the body in all senses. They are like huge insects, filled with lines and segments made to connect them to some perspective or other of nature of which they seem nothing more than a detached geometry. (*Théâtre*, p. 77)

10. The hieroglyph (and later, it will be seen, the analogy), does not quite operate as the flat abolition of duality as Sollers seems to suggest ("La pensée émet des signes," in *Logiques* (Paris: Editions du Seuil, 1968], p. 138), but rather as an endless concatenation of dualities and displacements that are the movement toward that abolition.

11. Repeatedly described in *The Theater and Its Double.*

12. The relationship between Soaemias and Séméion is discussed on page 82.

13. "I cite now an ancient historian who can say better than I could how he acted in fact in order to succeed the Antoinins." (p. 404)

14. Cf. the following commentary of J.-L. Brau, from *Antonin Artaud* (Paris: Le Table Ronde, 1971).

> Twenty years of frequenting the works of Artaud, biographical research in order to close in on him "on the track" have led me, for my part, to consider *Héliogabale* to be at the same time his reflected and projected image, that which he is and that which he wished to be.
> No doubt that Artaud identified himself with Héliogabale—but to what degree? (pp. 143-44)

15. "to tread: to copulate with—used of a male bird." *Webster's Seventh New Collegiate Dictionary.*

16. fiacre n.m. V. fiaque

fiaque and, by epenthesis, fiacre

n.m. behind. . . .

Dictionnaire historique des argots français (Paris: Larousse, 1965), p. 288.

17. *Dictionnaire d'histoire et de géographie ecclésiastiques* (Paris: Letouzey and Ané, 1912) 16: 1380-81.

18. Cf. "By that it is understood that poetry is anarchical to the extent that it places in question all the relationships of one object to another and of forms to their significations." (*Théâtre*, p. 62)

19. This and the following quotations are from Fabre d'Olivet, *De l'état social de l'homme*, I: 273, 274 respectively, cited by Thévenin, p. 421. They may be found in the English edition *Hermeneutic Interpretation of the Origin of the Social State of Man* (New York: G. P. Putnam's Sons, 1915), pp. 155-56.

20. Artaud compares this idiocy to the other form of reproduction or love as follows:

> And he who is thrown to the ground with the consciousness of an idiot . . . with just what he needs of consciousness in order to love . . . in a marvelous, spontaneous bound—who of love knows only the flame, the flame without radiance and without the multiplicity of the fire, he will have less than that other . . . for whom love is a thorough and horrible separation. (p. 61)

21. This *démarquage* explains a complex maneuver of Artaud in which he sets up the "War of Principles" as an originary, apparently historical state (very much as Nietzsche does Music) and then doubly presents the unfolding of myths or recorded history in the ages to come as the naive obliteration of the pagan sense for the cruel and double origin and as the very moment that brings about a doubling and therefore loss of an (apparently) previously integral origin.

22. See Robert Graves, *The Greek Myths* (London: Penguin, 1955), I: 184.

23. In view of its insistence on the operation of the *organe* (voice), on organization, both as system and as the unlimited articulation of analogy, and elsewhere in *Héliogabale* on the function of dismemberment, how can this essay be said to relate itself to Jacques Derrida's "La parole soufflée," in *L'écriture et la différence*, op. cit., a text whose main ploy (in a composition of endless ploys) is the apparent assertion of the very opposite.

> *L'organisation* est l'articulation, l'ajointement des fonctions ou des membres (ἄρθρον, artus) le travail et le jeu de leur differentiation. Celle-ci constitue à la fois la membrure et le démembrement de mon (corps) propre. Artaud redoute le corps articulé comme le mot d'un seul et même trait, pour une seule et même raison. (p. 279)

Héliogabale is a humorous reveling in—rather than the dread of—articulation. It is a text that, through its endless organ-ization approaches the limits of disorganization—organ-ized so absolutely that no element of articulation can establish a hierarchical position over another.

To be sure, we concede this as only one face of *Héliogabale*, just as Derrida doesn't fail to note that the dread of articulation is supplemented by "another facet of his text."

With one entire face of his discourse, he destroys a tradition that lives *in* difference, alienation, and negativity without seeing in it the origin and the necessity. To awaken this tradition, Artaud summons it back, in short, to his own motifs—self-presence [*présence à soi*], unity, self-identity, that which is one's own [*le propre*], etc. . . . But with another facet of his text, the most difficult one, Artaud affirms the *cruel* law, (that is to say, in the sense in which he understands this word, necessary), of difference—a law that is this time born by consciousness and no longer lived in metaphysical naiveté. (p. 291, op. cit.)

24. In "Le théâtre de la cruauté," anarchy and analogy, if not identical are at least analogous: " . . . these explosive interventions of a poetry and a humor entrusted with disorganizing and pulverizing appearances, according to the anarchical, analogical principle of all true poetry." (*Théâtre*, pp. 149f.)

25. A matrix of associations taken from passages on pp. 80 and 421 of vol. VII, *Oeuvres complètes*, cited on p. 73 of this text.

26. Séméion is both "*le* Séméion" and "*elle.*"

27. This and the previous passage were taken from "The Goddesse of Surrye," in *Lucian* (Cambridge: Harvard University Press, 1961), IV: 389 (first passage) and 353.

28. Cf.

The contemporary theater is decadent because it has lost all feeling on the one hand for the serious and on the other for laughter. Because it has broken with gravity, with immediate and pernicious efficacy—to sum it up—with Danger.

Because it has lost moreover the sense of true humor and of the physical and anarchical power of dissociation of laughter. (*Théâtre*, p. 51)

CHAPTER FOUR—BENJAMIN

. 1. All page references are to Walter Benjamin, "Zum Bilde Prousts," *Illuminationen* (Frankfurt: Suhrkamp, 1961). English translations are my own.

2. The German word *Bild* may refer to a picture, a portrait, or a metaphor. The title could best be translated "Towards the Image of Proust."

3. The earlier part of the passage indicates that similarity implies nonidentity: ". . . the deeper similarity of the dreamworld in which what takes place *never emerges as identical but only as similar*—impenetrably similar to itself" (p. 358, italics mine).

4. That remembrance, a temporal process, should play the role of time is hardly surprising: time functions here as a medium through which coincidence with past life is rendered possible. Why aging should play the role of space will become evident when, later in the passage, "aging" is seen to involve the forming of the image. A similar structure already appeared in the woven text description where "remembrance" and "forgetting" were counterposed. Remembrance, just as in the present passage, can be seen to figure as time. Since forgetting was called ornamentation and brought forth the spatial patterns of the woven carpet, it can be seen to figure as space.

5. Discussed on p. 93 of this essay.

6. Benjamin writes of forgetting: "Every morning, awakened, we hold in our hands, mostly weakly and loosely, only by a couple of fringes, the tapestry of lived existence as forgetting wove it in us" (p. 356).

7. See the passage cited on p. 98 of this essay.

8. We should no longer find it strange that the physiognomy functions as metaphor for the Proustian image. This terminology was carefully heralded twice before in the essay. First in the definition of Proust's image ("The image [*Bild*] of Proust is the highest physiognomic expression. . . ."), and later at the end of Part I of the essay: in Proust's world "the true surrealistic face of existence breaks through. To this [the world] belongs what takes place in Proust—and how carefully and elegantly it arises. Namely, never

isolatedly, lofty and visionary, but rather heralded and multiply supported, bearing a fragile, precious reality—the image" (p. 359).

9. As one passes from memory of life to the image in the passages already read and a fourth yet to be discussed, a vocabulary of time bound up with interiority and depth (*Erinnerung, Restauration des ursprünglichen* . . . , p. 356; *eingerollt, was drin liegt*, p. 365; *Innerste, Reflexion*, p. 356; *Innerste, innersten Schwingen, tiefste Schicht*, p. 368) gives way to a vocabulary of space, surface, texture, and a rising to the surface (*Weben*, p. 355; *Ornamente, verschlungener Arabesken*, p. 356; *entleeren*, p. 358; *auftauchen*, pp. 358f.; *zum Durchbruch kommen*, p. 359; *raumverschränkte, außen, Verschlingung, Vergegenwärtigung, Runzeln und Falten, Eintragungen*, p. 365; *Bild*, pp. 358, 359; *Züge, Gesichtsbilder, Gebilde, Bilder, diesen Fang zu heben*, p. 368).

The concept of time from which Benjamin distances himself is that of the conventional interpretation of Proust's *mémoire involontaire*, time as a medium for restoration through memory. A naive interpretation of time is presented which offers a deceptive promise of coincidence and unity in which the present moment seems capable of mirroring and re-presenting the past: but, with the ascendancy of the woven carpet of forgetting, with the passage to the dreamworld of nonidentity, and with the shock of aging, spatial difference (the *Bild*) is introduced and the coincidence of two points of time is shown as impossible. The particular roles played by time and space are somewhat arbitrary, and it would be false to conclude that the direction of movement in the passages—from time to space—implies a simple priority of space over time. The space-crossing of time indicates the movement in which discrepancy takes place and out of which the image emerges: this discrepancy is concerned rather with an intersection of the two than with a priority of either. And although it is not the case in Benjamin's essay, one could imagine another movement through which discrepancy takes place, a movement that proceeds from a naive concept of the spatial image into which temporal difference is introduced.

10. "Homesickness for the world distorted in the state of similarity, in which the true surrealistic face of existence breaks through. To it [this world] belongs what takes place in Proust. . . . bearing a fragile, precious reality—the image" (p. 359).

"Not reflection [*Reflexion*]—bringing to mind [*Vergegenwärtigung*] is Proust's method. He [Proust] is imbued with the truth that we all have no time to live the true dramas of existence that are allotted to us. That makes us age. Nothing else. The wrinkles and folds in our faces are the recordings [*Eintragungen*] of the great passions, of the vices, the knowledge [*Erkenntnisse*] that called on us" (pp. 365–56).

11. The "ornament" is the woven carpet of lived experience, yet demands the forgetting of life: both the stocking and Proust's dummy seem to represent a contents but turn out to be empty: the physiognomy is the record of past life, yet indicates our absence to that life.

12. It is here that we may see the preposition in Benjamin's title "Zum Bilde Prousts" as more significant than its apparent conventionality would suggest. The movement "towards" the image is never definitively completed.

13. Jacques Derrida's formulation is very similar to what takes place in Benjamin: "Without referring back to a 'nature,' the immotivation of the trace has always *become*. In fact, there is no unmotivated trace: the trace is indefinitely its own becoming-unmotivated." *Of Grammatology* (Baltimore: The Johns Hopkins University Press, 1976), p. 47.

14. The "new reality" which Benjamin speaks of here refers to his earlier description of the image as a "fragile, precious reality" (p. 359): and the movement away from reflection on life that brings about the traits of aging obviously recalls the formation of the image-physiognomy in the opening pages of Section III of the essay.

15. Although it is not within the scope of this essay, a more elaborate study of "Towards the Image of Proust" would take into account the complex play that Benjamin makes on specific passages of *À la recherche du temps perdu*. This particular description of Proust, for example, refers to the comparison between Michelangelo and Vinteuil in "La prisonnière," (Bruges: Bibliothèque de la Pléiade, 1954), III: 254-55.

16. "Torn by homesickness he lay on the bed. Homesickness for the world distorted in the state of similarity, in which the true surrealistic face of existence breaks through. To it [this world] belongs what takes place in Proust . . . the image" (pp. 358-59).

17. See the discussion on pp. 104-05.

CHAPTER FIVE—AFTERWORD

1. From *Webster's Seventh New Collegiate Dictionary* (Springfield: G. and C. Merriam, 1963), p. 460. See Paul Zumthor, "Jonglerie et language," *Poétique* 2 (1972): 321-36.

2. A translation of this short text may be found in the Appendix.

3. Joker

   n 1a: a person given to joking
       b: FELLOW
   2a: a playing card added to a pack as a wild card or as the highest-ranking card
       b(1): an ambiguous or apparently immaterial clause inserted in a legislative bill to make it inoperative or uncertain in some respect
         (2): an unsuspected, misleading, or misunderstood clause, phrase, or word in a document that nullifies or greatly alters it
       c: something held in reserve to gain an end or escape from a predicament
       d: an unsuspected or not readily apparent fact, factor, or condition that thwarts or nullifies a seeming advantage

(From *Webster's Seventh New Collegiate Dictionary*, op. cit., p. 458).

4. Baudelaire, *Oeuvres complètes* (Bruges: Bibliothèque de la Pléiade, 1964), pp. 269-73.

5. Until reading the alibi, the juggler had always read the ball/text as concealing a secret, had always known that the secret of the ball/text was alibi—elsewhere—ultimately in the control of the other.

Library of Congress Cataloging in Publication Data
Jacobs, Carol.
    The dissimulating harmony.

    1. Symbolism in literature. I. Title.
PN56.S9J3   809'.91'5   77-18392
ISBN 0-8018-2040-5